MW01228718

The Magical Héroes

Book 1

The Little Girl and the Pope

Claudia Carbonell

Claudia Carbonell

Claudia Carbonell

The Little Girl and the Pope
Claudia Carbonell

Claudia Carbonell

Dedication

To Pope Francis and to the Harr Family

Claudia Carbonell

A portion of the proceeds from the sales of this book
will go to ending child slavery

http://www.freetheslaves.net/

Claudia Carbonell

"If life gives you lemons, change the world!"

Vivienne Harr (12 years old)

A Facebook message I sent to Vivienne Harr on November 11, 2016, when she and her family were heading to the Peace Summit at the Vatican:

Most likely my dear friends, the Harr Family, will be in Rome when they receive this. WELCOME TO BEAUTIFUL ROME!

Pasta al dente, tomato with roasted garlic and basil sprinkled with balsamic vinegar and extra virgin olive oil awaits your taste buds.

Inno Impero Romano is playing. Your eyes and your family's will be set on the Marthae Domus Sanctae shining brightly under the glorious sun.

Your steps advancing ever more briskly, excited... impatient.

Changing the world can't wait unnecessary seconds.

Those children agonizing under the burning sun, with empty tummies, lifting rocks on their achy shoulders double their weight anxiously await for a little girl to tell their stories to a holy man who will listen. Who will understand the story of those children? Who will give them a bit of comfort, a semblance of childhood and some needed hope?

A little girl and a holy man are about to come together and the world rejoices. Children sing. Angels celebrate. The earth trembles expecting, anticipating a most welcome Seed. This Seed is to be planted in the most fertile grounds that exist: inside people's hearts. It will sprout into Love and it will eventually grow into the awesome tree of compassionate Deeds.

This novel is based on true events.

Claudia Carbonell

The Gahate village in the Sindhupalchok district of Nepal extends upwards, like a rustic manger with tiny half-built houses, inhabited by large families and animals that share the dwellings, surrounded by vast terrain and fragrant spruces that give a Western Christmas feel.

The dirt road that leads to the village scratches the edges of a mountain which has robbed land of its existence and spirals upwards to arrive at the uneven, fragrant, and charming grounds.

Although the village lacks comfortable homes, it compensates with a peaceful atmosphere. The view all around it, upwards and downwards, is populated by mountains, pines, huge sunflowers, and people with friendly faces bringing wood to their homes, cutting sugar cane, stacking straw, breaking stones with thick hammers, cooking in open wood stoves, and collecting water from the stream that forges its way down the steep mountain.

At certain levels, the village is divided into cliffs where daring falls of crystalline water throw themselves to nourish the streams of the land below. In the mornings, the sky embraces Gahate with its misty mantle. As you gaze down, it seems as if you can walk on a cloud carpet. Winter turns the village white. The cold is intense. It freezes the bones and burns the skin.

Today was one of those times of chattering teeth. Aatish and Ballabh were rubbing their backs under their old denim tent and hugging their knees. They breathed through their mouths to warm their hands.

Their mom and Granny were lying at their feet, beneath another old tent that had belonged to their grandfather. He had died three years ago due to hypothermia. They had wandered for half a century around every village of Nepal until three years ago when Granny decided to leave the difficult life of a nomad and built a house of her own for her grandchildren. Gahate was almost the ideal place.

"Are you awake, Mommies? "Ballabh asked.

There was no answer. Aatish knew they were pretending to be asleep. He was clever. After all, he had turned nine years old four months ago and it allowed him to see what his brother could not see at seven years of age.

Their grandmother, especially, seemed to be very strong, but everyone knew of her strange illness.

"Granny is pretending to be asleep," Aatish affirmed. "She thinks she can fool us, but I've heard her coughing. Every time she did, she bled. She discreetly covered her mouth with an old handkerchief which had belonged to the grandfather or stepped out of the house to spit it out.

In Gahate, the word *doctor* or *hospital* were myths brought by Western tourists. They, like the Greeks and their mythologies, knew nothing else than to invent stories.

Finally, when the extreme fatigue was stronger than the cold, the Singh family fell asleep.

The clucking of Dafir, the family's rooster, awakened them. He jumped to the side of the window and fluttered hard. His six-hen harem and he required food.

Aatish took his torn sandal and threw it at the window. The broken glass was upholstered with a piece of cardboard which he had taped there three months ago when the weather turned cold.

"Darn bird, it always wakes me up!" yelled Aatish. He was the one who slept the least of the family since he felt cold the most. *It's probably as a result of being born prematurely,* Granny thought, therefore it also justified his moodiness, rebellion, and disobedience. His preference of doing nothing was just a sign of how important he would be one day, of course, with proper education.

Coughing and covering her mouth with the handkerchief, Granny crawled out of the tent.

"Mother, go back to bed, it's very cold," Karishma insisted.

"My dear, I don't do any good heating up the bed," she said. "Besides you must be hungry. I'll go and check the nests to see how many eggs we have and I'll feed the poor hens. Just listen to Dafir's insistence for us to take care of them," she said laughing.

"I'll go with you, Grandma," Ballabh offered, creeping out from under the tent. Karishma also climbed out of her canvas.

"Thank you, little one," she answered. "You, Aatish, stay in bed. Do not hurry," she insisted, taking her tent and spreading it over him. It was one of his great delights, to stay in bed with double blankets in the winter and, in the summer, to jump in the brook with his brother as soon as the rough fabric of his bed made his skin itch.

Grandma always brought broth to the shore while they were swimming.

When they got tired, they raced through the meadow and joined other neighborhood children and played tag or chased after hens.

Everything they did were great feats for Granny and Mom. They had been nomads all their lives and knew only work, setting up their tents in the most inclement places, and hiking for endless miles. Their grandmother was a typical nomad with thick calluses on her feet that allowed her to walk barefoot and to save the expense of a pair of sandals. The cracks on the toes and on the edges of her heels were unsightly but to be expected.

She had already washed the six eggs for breakfast and milked the goat. Now, she was about to fetch a pail of water from the brook, bring it to the wood stove that Karishma, with the help of Ballabh, had set alight.

Coming up the winding road and raising dirt, Devang, an elegant businessman and philanthropist of Pokhara, was approaching in his luxurious truck. Granny rushed to a pine tree where she took a handful of water and washed her face, sprinkled some on her hair, and with her fingers untangled it as best she could. She poured water on her feet and rubbed them together to clean off the dirt. She had to look her best.

The truck came to a halt next to the house with dust flying past it and into everyone's eyes. The grandmother coughed and spat blood beside the pine.

Excited, she hurried to meet the great gentleman, all the while continuing looking down as it was not appropriate to gaze at his face.

"Welcome! The good God has brought you to this humble village," she remarked breathlessly. Karishma bent and lifted her head. Ballabh bowed as Aatish was coming out of the house, rubbing his eyes.

"Are you just getting up, son, while your family works?" asked Devang while getting out of the vehicle. All of him flashed luxury, starting with his gold-fringed pearly teeth and his clothing, including his thick-soled shoes that were as white as angels' clothing.

"Yes, I just got up. What do you care?" Aatish said between his teeth. Granny was the only one who understood him as she read the movement of his lips.

"The boy is not feeling well, sir," replied their grandmother, looking at his shoes and wondering, *Who could have been the artisan responsible for such a fine work of art?* "I'll bring you a stool," she offered, heading to the house.

"It's not necessary, madam. Please stay since I do not have much time," he replied. I'm just passing by and in a great hurry." He gave a long stare at the boys. Their grandmother and mom only listened to his musical words while the brothers observed him closely, Ballabh with much joy while Aatish with some disdain. Aatish thought it was ridiculous to dress so extravagantly to visit a village such as theirs.

He contrasted starkly with their plain clothes, lack of shoes, and primitive surroundings.

A crowd of people encircled the vehicle and touched it as if it were a jewel. Ballabh wished to join them but thought it was imprudent. The gentleman addressed his words to all of them.

Since last winter, the great lord had visited the village and others in the neighborhood and had brought clothes, sandals, blankets, ready-made food in cans, and a sharp tool to open them. Because of him, many had tasted the most delicious soups. He was revered by all. His goodness knew no bounds.

"I came to bring you good news," he announced, and turned to face the crowd that had gathered around his truck. "Whoever wants to ride in my vehicle, please do so. My belongings are yours, kind Gahate." He turned his gaze to the Singh brothers, "Today, I'm bringing something better than gifts. I bring you the proposition of a bright future for the forthcoming generation. What do you think children of studying in the best schools of Pokhara? To become illustrious men and women? I owe my bright future to a gentleman who gave me this same opportunity." He studied the expression of the eyes of mothers, especially the grandmothers. "Today is my wish to return the favor to the person who changed my life."

Granny's hands were shaking so much that the eggs ended up on the ground while the pail of water landed upside down on her feet.

Approximately seven thousand miles away, drops of water poured over a busy road and atop two hurried pedestrians. They were heading to a museum.

The museums were among Vivienne's favorite places. Taking her father Eric's hand, she tried to keep up with his strides. For each one of his steps, she made three and a jump since her legs could not compare to her father's. He was six feet five inches tall. He was a champion. In his first triathlon race. he had won sixth place in the world then won forty more races. He was one of the best triathletes in the United States and, as if that wasn't enough, he was also a great author of sports and business books.

"We're almost there, princess," affirmed her father.

"Oh, that's good!" She replied, though she would be a thousand times more excited if her little brother Turner had accompanied them. But he did not like museums. Unlike him, Vivienne was fascinated by them. As an artist, it was important to know the art of others and to learn from them. She had learned a lot from her favorite artist, her mom Alexandra Harr.

She painted beautiful watercolor landscapes and each of her works were inspired by the surroundings and history of where they lived in Pleasanton, California.

Such was the case of the Eylar Mountain that framed Pleasanton. It stood 4,089 feet tall and was topped by a two-story wooden tower. Her mother had painted it in emerald, gold and mahogany. To the sides she had painted the ravines that bathed it: the Colorado, Sycamore, Pino, and Dry, in indigo, teal, and – in Vivienne's favorite color – turquoise. Her mother had explained that Eylar was the fourth highest mountain in Santa Clara, California, and her father used to climb it – until recently. Since then, it turned out the mountain had an owner and he had forbidden people to climb it since he did not want to share it with anyone.

It was as unfair since it was dumb for mountains to have owners, Vivienne thought each time she rested her gaze on the mountain.

The museum was in front of them. Its facade of fairy-tale cottage was as cozy as the colonial architecture of the mid-1800s. At its entrance stood Luma, the pretty Indian girl who was handing out information pamphlets of the museum exhibits.

"This month, on the second floor, we have the black-and-white photography exhibition of renowned photographer, Lisa Kristine," Luma explained, handing them brochures.

"Princess," said Eric, "would you like to first see the photographic exhibition and leave the paintings for last?"

"All right, Dad. Thanks, Luma," Vivienne said as she ran up the stairs.

"Careful, princess, don't run so fast!" Eric warned and jumped up two stairs to land beside her. His hand was soft, yet firm. In case she stumbled against some object, he was always ready to grab her before she fell.

Vivienne had been prone to falls. The scars on her knees and arms were testimony of it as were the mockery of her schoolmates who thought it was very funny every time she fell. "Clumsy," was the word they used most each time Vivienne lost balance and ended up on the floor.

She would usually come home with her stomach knotted from the shame she felt when she was regarded as dumb. She was not! It just so happened that the floor of the school playground, and others as well, was uneven and made her plummet.

Once when she was hurrying to her room, the floor curled up and tossed her sideways into the wall. Her mother, who was coming out of her bedroom, witnessed it. Immediately, she made an appointment with the ophthalmologist and Vivienne left the office with thick glasses.

Since then, the mockery had worsened. Her new nickname was "Miss Magu," taken from the near-sighted character of Mr. Magu. That character had nothing in common with her!

However, when you are eight years old and you're compared to an earthworm, each time you look at the mirror you can't help noticing some features of the critter.

They had already reached the second floor. In front of them were the luxuriously framed photos.

Too bad they're not in color, thought Vivienne, gazing at a photograph of the San Francisco Bridge. In real life, it was painted red like her mother's favorite lipstick, but in the photo it appeared gray. There was also a picture of a man whose face was tangled with wrinkles.

When she stationed herself in front of the picture next to the old man's and fixed her gaze upon it, she felt a lump in her throat. As she swallowed, her heart dove to her belly. In front of her was an image that was impossible to conceive. It was more unheard of than her being compared to a ridiculous cartoon character or a critter!

That photograph showed a pair of children carrying two massive rocks tied behind their backs. Due to their cargo's overwhelming weight, belts were tied to their heads to help balance the weight. Their huge shoes were better suited for a big man like her dad.

One wrong step, the children would fall, and ...

"Oh no!" She shouted. Her dad jumped up to her side. Vivienne suddenly felt the sum total of all the mockery she had endured ever since the first grade. What she called *not feeling valued.*

"What is it, princess?" he shouted, taking her by the shoulders.

"Dad, look at these kids!" she cried, raising the volume of her voice and moving her glasses up to the bridge of her nose. She had to make sure what she was seeing. Many times, her eyes showed her uneven floors while everyone saw them as perfectly level.

"Why do these kids have such big shoes? Do you see, Daddy, what lies in front of them?" The boys were standing on the cliff of a mountain. "Dad, if these children take one wrong step, they would fall into the cliff! Why are they not at school? Why are they carrying such heavy stones? Look at how their shoulders slump because of the weight!" She wailed, feeling a burst of fire burning in her belly.

She felt the same way the day she went to the circus. Unfortunately, the memory was as fresh as if it had been yesterday. She was four years old and her parents took her to the Ringling Brothers and Barnum and Bailey Circus. She was happy to see her mom so excited. "It will be an unforgettable experience for Vivi," she repeated.

The first act was a delight. A trapeze artist dressed in a shimmering pink bathing suit, was thrown from the top. Another acrobat, wearing a suit made of the same shiny material, threw himself on the opposite side and took her hands. However, the second act was disastrous. Seven elephants took the stage followed by their trainer. He wore white clothing and clenched a club. He shouted an order and threw them a blow, making the elephants stand on their hind legs.

Then, he made them sit on the ground, lay down, back up and ended the act strolling with each holding the others' tails with their trunks.

That act was not only disrespectful to the elephants since it was unnatural to their species, but it was also cruel. They were slaves for the pleasure of Man.

In that moment, she remembered a book that Joaquina, her nanny read to her every day; *The Magical House*, by Claudia... she couldn't remember her last name. It was about abused animals and what they felt.

That image was as disturbing as the picture in front of her. As a bonus, it had a name equally devastating: *"Child slaves,"* Vivienne read it aloud.

"What do they mean by slaves?" she asked. She knew the world had malaria and poor people, but slaves? "Weren't they freed by Abraham Lincoln?" She had learned about the sixteenth president of the United States in the third grade. He established the Emancipation Proclamation to free the slaves in the United States. Although not all were released, it led to the Thirteenth Amendment of the Constitution. A few years later, on January 31, 1865, Congress finally accepted it. But it was not until December 6, 1865, that Congress finally authorized it, eight months after Lincoln's death.

"No, princess," replied her dad. "I hate to tell you that there are still many slaves around the world."

"What? How many are there?" Vivienne's eyes began to water, and her blue eyes turned turquoise. Eric pulled his cell phone from his trouser pocket and began to search. Meanwhile, Vivienne was still in a trance, watching the painting while hugging her abdomen with both hands.

The sting persisted from the picture that, although it was tormenting her, she could not help but stare at it. It seemed like those horrendous car accidents that you feel horrified when you witness them, yet you can't tear your eyes away from them.

"According to Google, there are 18 million child slaves in the world."

"18 million? That is too many." All her surroundings began to spin. The floor swelled up in spite of her glasses being well adjusted. She took her father's hand.

"Princess, are you crying?"

She had not noticed her tears since the bewilderment of seeing those two children contemplating the cliff. Their images had been nailed to her heart.

Perhaps they were considering the possibility of jumping and ending their sad existence. At the same time, she enjoyed freedom, two loving parents, and a brother. Although he was sometimes mischievous, she loved him with all her heart. As for these children, did they have parents? Were they loved? They definitely had no joy or fun, and certainly no toys. Most overwhelming, they had no freedom.

"Dad, those children must be at school, or playing, not carrying heavy rocks on their backs. Those slabs are at least double their weight!"

"You're right, my love. This is very sad."

"It is," she agreed, heading for a bench in front of the picture that was now twisting her view of life.

She moved slowly as if she was carrying those heavy rocks on her shoulders and the strap tied to her head was flattening her. The distorted floor and the spinning room did not help to keep her balanced.

When she sat down, she recognized that her father had also taken a seat next to her. She stared at the painting. It looked very unfocused. Tears had blurred her vision of it.

"It breaks my heart to see you cry," he said.

"I can't help it," she admitted, her throat tightening. "What are we going to do, Dad?" When she visited the circus at four years of age and witnessed the abuse of the elephants, she cried and her parents immediately took her hand and left. This time, she could not escape the reality of child slavery. She had to face up to it and change it.

"Princess, what can we do to help those slave boys?"

"Free them, Dad! We must free them!" They went silent. Once Vivienne's vision had cleared, her eyes had dried and the showroom had stopped spinning, her mind obeyed her will to ask a question. It insisted on a number and it had to be exact. "How much money is needed to free all the slave children of the world?"

Eric took out his cell phone again. He knew that every time Vivienne asked a question, she did not stop until she got an answer. Again, he turned to Google for a rough estimate since the world's most sophisticated Internet searcher had no exact answer.

"It takes approximately $150,000 to free about 500 slaves."

Vivienne's face brightened. She jumped to her feet. "Very well, I will free them," she replied. "I promise to release you," she continued, approaching the photo. She slid her index finger over the thick black frame of the picture. *Someone has to take care of you,* she thought.

As Eric drove back home, he gave Vivienne several fun proposals. He was determined to distract his daughter from her silent and intense frown.

"Shall we go to Cherry on Top, for yoghurt?" was the first proposition. The invitation did not even slightly move her. "Oh, there's a great movie. It's called, *How to Train Your Dragon.* Do you want to see it?" He asked and gazed at her again.

Her frown was still as puckered as before and her eyes, magnified by the thick glasses, seemed fixed on the Eylar Mountain.

She's tired, her father thought. *As soon as she gets home, she'll play with Turner and forget about the museum.* Turner was now five years old. When she was about to turn four, they asked her what she wanted for her birthday and she replied, "A sister."

Turner was born the next year and it was the best thing that could have ever happened to her. Her brother was on par with Mother Teresa of Calcutta and Pope Francis. In addition, Turner was bright, playful, funny, and her best friend.

He got upset when kids made fun of her. He wanted to grow up fast so he could go to school with her and put them in their place. He said he would do it with a clean fist, although his parents did not approve of violence.

"No one messes with my sister," Turner insisted in a menacing voice. This year, they had started going to school together and everything was better. Well, sort of. The school bullies didn't listen to Turner. They continued with their mockery. Vivienne's acting skills helped her to pretend to be calm even though she was under a lot of pressure, now more than ever due to her discovery that there were child slaves.

Eric turned to their street, Harmony Lane. As they passed over the narrow wooden bridge, Vivienne glanced down at the stream below them, running as fast as her thoughts. As she lifted her face, she was now in front of the gate of her home. The house could not be seen from the outside due to the thick branches of four Catalpa trees that tucked it away from view.

The lawn in the front yard seemed to be covered with snow. They were the Catalpa flowers that looked like orchids and their sweet scent accented their beauty. In the background, on either side of the stairs which led to the porch, there was an arched gazebo surrounded by climbing red roses. They contrasted with the whiteness on the ground and provided a Christmas touch, which was funny since the month of May had just started.

As soon as Eric drove the car into the garage, Vivienne opened the door and jumped out before her dad even stepped on the brake.

Fast as a bullet, she dashed to the door of the house, shouting, "Mommy! Mommy!"

Uff, uff, uff. Buddy, her 46-pound Labradoodle, pounced on her. As he placed his paws on her chest, he stretched to his maximum height of 20 inches and prepared to lick her face. But this time, she pushed him away.

"Baby!" Alexandra jumped from behind the refrigerator. There was a stench of something burning. Vivienne knew she had probably burnt something on the stove or, with luck, just the iron. "My Gosh, what happened to your dad?" she asked and hurried to the garage door.

"Daddy's okay, Mommy, what's not is..." at that moment Eric barged in looking as if a pail of flour had fallen on his face.

Buddy went ballistic with excitement at the sight of his master. He began running back and forth from the door to the kitchen when he sensed the tension.

"Missy, you got out of the car while it was still moving. That's very dangerous. Don't ever do that again, OK?" He sniffed the air and chose not to ask what the scent was.

"Is Turner all right?" He asked raising his voice.

"He is beaming. Today he beat me at Chinese Checkers," answered Alexandra.

"I'm sorry, Daddy, for jumping out of the car," Vivienne said, "but there's no time to lose." She continued running to the kitchen. Having jumped out of the car was strange since she never took any risks. She had only agreed to ride the rollercoaster in Knotts Berry Farm four months ago because Turner insisted she go with him.

"Daddy, while you were driving, I came up with an idea," she declared as she climbed up the kitchen counter and took a bag of lemons from the basket of fruit.

"I'll make lemonade to sell and free the child slaves." Her parents stared at each other and their jaws dropped. With mouths wide open they said, "What?"

"Mommy," Vivienne continued as she untied the knot from the mesh bag that held a dozen lemons and tossed them into the sink.

"Did you know that there are child slaves in the world?"

"Of course, my little girl. It's a very sad thing," Alexandra replied.

"Dad said the same thing and yet neither of you have done anything about it."

She grabbed a cleaning rag from the drawer where Alexandra kept the most varied collection of fabrics for the kitchen. At their best times, they had been the family's clothing. With a piece of one of Alexandra's former wool skirts, she dried the lemons.

She took a knife from the drawer where her mother had strictly forbidden her children to open. Only she and Eric were allowed to do so.

"What do you want to do with that knife, missy?" Eric's voice sounded more grave than before. Instantly, he jumped to her side before she cut herself.

Uff, uff! Buddy barked, wanting to impose order as he stood between Eric and Vivienne. His abundant, thick chocolate-colored hair looked like sheep's wool that required pruning every month since it grew so much and made him look like a huge furry ball. Such was his current appearance.

"I must practice several lemonade recipes because I need to collect $150,000 to free the child slaves in the world."

Eric and Alexandra gazed at their daughter's face. In her eyes, there was so much hope. It had the glow of unwavering faith.

What right do I have to take away such a beautiful idea? Eric thought, although he was considering the possibility of taking his daughter to an ear doctor. In addition to having acute myopia, her ears were failing. It seems she heard that with $150,000, she would free all 18 million slave children, but he had told her that this sum would only free 500.

My little girl is so strange. There is so much empathy in her, Alexandra thought, considering she should be evaluated by a psychologist.

"Dad, do you remember the book you bought me at Barnes and Noble, written by Pope Francis entitled, *God's Name Is Mercy?*" Indeed, Eric remembered it.

One Sunday afternoon, after leaving church, they had visited the library and Eric asked the kids to choose a book. Eric was surprised at Vivienne's choice.

"He says," she continued, "Mercy is not mercy if there is no action. I want to do what God asks of us: to have mercy for others."

For much of the night, Vivienne and Alexandra squeezed lemons until their wrists and palms were sore from leaning them so much against the electric presser. Twice, Turner accompanied his dad to the supermarket to buy two dozen more lemons and a couple more ingredients that they did not have at home: raw agave nectar and cayenne pepper. Vivienne insisted on exhausting all sorts of flavors for her lemonade even if they were spicy like peppers.

After several trials and ingesting so much lemonade to the point that her palate could not withstand any more, Vivienne decided on the winning recipe. It was to be lemons, water, a little ice and agave nectar for sweetening. It was the perfect concoction to lure a bunch of thirsty people in search of a delicious and nutritious drink that would serve the noblest cause of all.

"Now I'm going to need a lemonade stand. Daddy, you're going to build it for me. Yes!" This was not a request but an excited order.

An order Eric would have to obey since it was for such a noble cause. Plus, *Who could say no to Vivienne? Besides, it would be a fun hobby for her,* he thought.

That Friday at dawn, when everyone went to sleep, Eric turned on the computer to search for lemonade stands. The choices were too expensive. They did not have the budget for such an item. Moreover, Alexandra assured him, Vivienne would soon drop the idea of freeing child slaves. "After all, she is just a little girl."

The next day, the kids' tree house was covered with a blanket of mist. The day was perfect to spend it there. Atop of two robust apple trees, Vivienne and Turner had built their play house. Dad had added a ton of nails to the walls, the floor, to secure it over the tree. The kids had done the most important work; they laid their sleeping bags and installed two headboards to allow their bags to look like real beds. They had decorated it with their mom's old lamp and several pictures painted by Alexandra and Vivienne.

The house felt like a gigantic and comfortable nest surrounded by windows. They could stick out their hands to grab apples. If they fancied something different to eat, Alexandra asked them to throw down the elevator, which was a basket that she filled with food.

"Bye, kids," their dad shouted, "I'm going to Home Depot, will you join me?" Turner would have loved to go, but he chose to stay because he knew Vivienne did not like that store.

For hours, they planned and played about selling lemonade and freeing the slaves. Buddy nodded at the idea.

When they were beginning to feel hungry, their mother called, "Kids, throw down the elevator." Turner grabbed the wicker basket and tossed it out the window. Vivienne stuck her face out, looking hopefully to see if there was going to be a box of pizza inside the basket. Instead, it was a dish covered with the usual aluminum lid. Alexandra served food luxuriously although her cuisine didn't merit it.

"Guys, eat around the edges, it's the center that's burnt."

"Oh, no, she cooked!" Turner whined.

"Babies, did you say something?"

"No, Mom, thank you," Vivienne replied. The pancakes were scorched and syrup-free.

"Really?" Turner grumbled.

"I'll convince her to order pizza."

They slid from the tree house on the slide with Buddy on his tail sandwiched between them and kicking the air until his paws touched the ground. They sprinted to the endless land behind their property. It was a forest; the perfect place to discard all food cooked by Mom.

They peered around, on the lookout for an animal interested in burnt pancakes. Miranda, the deer who once in a while visited their property, wasn't in view.

They discarded their breakfast behind the fence and Vivienne was pleased to see three nutcrackers, two long-beaked phalarope, and a canary ready to find out just how appetizing two black blobs could be. Buddy sniffed the breakfast and stepped back.

They hurried back home. Fortunately, Dad had returned with Chinese food for everyone. The next day, after church, they had lunch at Caspian, the fine Persian restaurant, and for dinner they had Greek food.

Claudia Carbonell

The best gift for the villagers of Gahate had been Devang's visit. The great lord had promised a better future for the young boys of the village. He would take them to Pokhara, the most educated city of Nepal, where they would go to school. The parents were elated. However, most kids only wanted to visit Pokhara and return back to their village with their families.

"We must sacrifice ourselves for the wellbeing of our children," insisted Granny who spoke faster and interrupted more often than the rest of the other villagers. With this method, she had persuaded her husband to leave their nomad lifestyle and settle in the village permanently.

"But Grandma, Ballabh and I don't want to leave," insisted Aatish. "We can't leave the village or be away from you!" Karishma studied their faces. There was so much joy in them, yet Granny saw the potential of a bright future for them through proper education.

"Children, imagine what it would be like to learn to read and write," she responded. "Think of the amount of knowledge you could acquire through reading the works of intelligent people!

It would be as if you were absorbing their life's experiences and their knowledge."

People wondered where their grandmother got so much wisdom. She spoke with eloquence and conviction. It seemed as if she had studied, but she never had.

Every time a donated book or an old newspaper arrived in the village, she rescued them. She would place it on the floor, close her eyes and run her fingers over the letters as if she was absorbing the information. Once she had distilled the wisdom from the written pages, she piled them atop the hay, cardboard boxes, and other written materials to help pad the beds of the family.

"If I had gone to school, I would have been a teacher," she assured, "and I would have taught all of you." She looked at her grandchildren. She restrained her cough by clearing her throat. At this moment, she could not go away to spit elsewhere since her motivational message was more urgent. "Mr. Devang promised to return you guys every month. We will not leave this village. We will be waiting here for you until the day you return," she affirmed.

Their grandmother coughed discreetly into her handkerchief all night. The next morning, Dafir, as usual, flew to the window sill and sang. This time, Aatish did not protest. He had not slept all night and was not sleepy. His grandmother had finally stopped coughing.

Karishma stepped out from under the tent and whispered, "Let's be quiet. Granny has finally fallen asleep. I'll go to the nest to collect eggs."

Ballabh crawled from under his tent as Aatish kept his gaze fixed on the ceiling at the back of the house. It was broken and he could see the roof tiles. The rain and the wind had knocked off part of the roof and ceiling. Although a wall divided both parts of the dwelling, the one in the back was destined for the goat and at one time it had also sheltered the cow that had died of old age.

"Mommy," whispered Ballabh, "I'm going to milk the goat."

"I'm coming with you," Aatish offered, creeping out of the tent. It was the first time in his ten years that he had offered to do a job. Had she been awake, his grandmother would have urged him to stay in bed, for he, being born prematurely at almost seven months, was not as strong as his younger brother.

They stepped out of the house and, while they were turning toward the second door and the barn, they saw the lights of Devang's truck in the distance blazing the mountain road, advancing in their direction.

"It's the rich gentleman!" shouted Ballabh, beaming with joy and thinking about all the possible gifts he could bring to the village.

"I'm going to wake up Grandma," he said as he hurried to the front door.

Aatish froze, staring at the trucks' headlights and the dust rising from the road. The mist faded the view of the stream where his Mom probably would be collecting water.

The sky was painted pink with lilac stripes. Peace rocked the village soothingly. Aside from the lights of the truck, Aatish couldn't see more than the immediate surroundings of his house. He raced through the front door eager to talk to his grandmother. It was very urgent for her to realize that it was not his desire to leave the village with a stranger.

He barged in. His mother was gazing out the window, holding Ballabh on her lap. She was crying.

"Mom, why are you crying?" asked Aatish.

"I'm going to miss you a lot, children."

"No, Momma, that's what I came to tell Grandma and you. I do not want to go away with that guy!"

"I know and I would like to be with you forever." She lifted Ballabh with one arm and took Aatish's hand and gently pulled him out the door. "But more important than my happiness is your future."

The truck was already in front of them. They closed their eyes. The bright lights blinded them and made their mother's tears burst free even more.

To Vivienne, a week had never seemed so long! "It's only seven days," she reasoned. She had calculated how many minutes there were in it: ten thousand and eighty. During those seven days, her father had seen several YouTube videos of people building food and drink stands. He had paused on his favorite videos after each sentence to write down every detail. He printed it and read and reread all the instructions.

Finally, on the ninth day, and with the help of Turner, the lemonade stand was finished. No doll, not even her finest dress, had looked more exquisite to her than this stand.

There was no time to lose! At 5:48 on a Monday morning, with Buddy at her side, she had already squeezed the lemons, added the water and the agave nectar with a little ice into the large glass jug. She had placed disposable cups, a pack of napkins, and extra lemons (for those who preferred the lemonade to be more sour) into the fruit basket.

Alexandra hurried to the kitchen, wrapping herself in her lavender robe.

"What are you doing, baby?" she asked and looked around to see if there was something out of order. She found several things in terrible disorder: the knife drawer open with a knife (no less) inside the sink; the lemonade made; the pile of fruit scattered on the kitchen counter; and the fruit basket filled with tiny cups, napkins and lemons.

Alexandra frowned. She preferred when the house remained immaculate. "It was sacred," she repeated many times. They had moved there when Vivienne was only six months old. Turner had been born in their room. It was also the most magical little house in the neighborhood. It was the result of Eric's entire athletic endeavor; of his endless hours of practice, sweat, pain, and perseverance. For Alexandra, their home represented her family memories and daily work as an artist.

"You cut the lemons," she said visibly upset. It was weird when something perturbed her. "That's my job."

Buddy started to lick her feet as if sensing her distress. *Any other mom would complain about the kitchen mess,* Vivienne thought. *Mine is only concerned about my safety.* She would have never had this realization had it not been for the photograph of those two child slaves.

"I'm sorry, Mommy," she said. *Who would care for child slaves? Surely it won't be their owners, because if they did, they would be free,* she thought.

Vivienne realized that her mother was talking to her, but she was not listening. She was absorbed in her thoughts.

"Wait for me a few seconds. I'm going to put on something appropriate to help you take the stand out," whispered Alexandra. She left on tippy toes. Vivienne thought her mother was a fairy. Many times, she had to adjust her glasses while watching her mom for she seemed to float above the floor. She was so beautiful, vibrant, and graceful. In addition, she was bright. Although she messed up when doing laundry, ironing, and cooking, she more than compensated with everything else. She was almost perfect.

Vivienne was pushing the stand towards the front door when she heard her mother's voice:

"Wait, baby, let me help you." She was wearing a green dress dotted with lemons which seemed to leap out of the fabric. She had yellow sandals with a bouquet of rhinestones on top of the toes. Only her mom could look so perfect in the morning. She was the envy of the ladies in the neighborhood who required hours of grooming to look like Alexandra's shadow on her worst day.

"Mommy, you look divine!" she said raising one end of the wooden stand. Alexandra took the opposite side and rushed to the front door.

Vivienne cheerfully followed. She was prepared for this special day. Her backpack and sweater were ready on the side bench. She was wearing her favorite jeans and a Snoopy-print blouse that Dad had bought for her at Knotts Berry Farm last year.

Buddy grabbed his leash between his teeth and handed it to Vivienne. Once she tightened it around his neck, Alexandra opened the door.

Outside, a blanket of mist covered the garden. Hundreds of birds were flying from tree to tree and were tweeting a lively conversation. The white flower carpet of the Catalpa trees covered the dew-covered lawn and the narrow cobblestone path from the front door to the gate.

"Slide your feet so you won't slip," Alexandra advised. Dragging their feet and lifting a bunch of white flowers, they reached the gate. Buddy skidded with every step he took. In front of the house, they installed the stand. They both stared at each other and giggled like little girls. Excitement tickled their tummies.

Her mother had told her that when she was pregnant with her, she used to read Dr. Seuss books every evening. She did it at night because she knew her baby would have a big smile during the hours of sleep when Alexandra stopped talking to her. Since then, they shared that special connection of feeling happy emotions at the same time.

They returned home to collect their product: the magnificent pitcher with the liberating elixir and the basket with lemons.

Alexandra insisted on taking the lemonade since it was heavy. She placed it in the middle of the stand, fixed her artist's gaze on it and decided to move it to one end. She pushed the basket to the other end.

"I'll be back," she said and hurried to the house. She returned with her jewelry box, a fine case covered in black suede, and placed it on a shelf underneath the stand.

"We'll put the money in here, little one," Alexandra proposed, opening the case.

"What did you do with your jewelry, Mommy?"

"For the moment it's on top of my dressing table," she replied, pulling Vivienne's glasses off. Suddenly, everything became cloudy. Alexandra smothered the glasses with her breath and wiped them with the hem of her dress.

"We'll sell all the lemonade, you'll see," she assured, putting her daughter's glasses back in place. Although Vivienne would've preferred to have continued with blurred vision, as the school bus was approaching. Her stomach immediately tied up in knots.

"Why is the bus coming so early?" asked Vivienne. Alexandra pulled her cell phone out of her dress pocket.

"Vivi, it's quarter to eight! How did time fly? Oh no! I have to get Turner ready!" Alexandra shouted, sliding back home.

Buddy went berserk barking not knowing whether to stay with Vivienne or to follow Alexandra.

Meanwhile Vivienne was stunned. *How will the school kids react when they see me with my lemonade stand outside my house?* This and many other thoughts crossed her mind. The most terrible one was if she would survive. *I'm sure they'll kill me!* She thought. The strange thing was that just now she thought about it. *How come I had not realized the consequences of having my stand for all to see?*

The ground was beginning to shrink and the school bus changed its square shape for the head of a dragon. With all her strength, she wished the bus engine to break down before it reached her house, allowing her to take the stand back home. But instead, as if it were a bullet, the bus shot its way toward her, tearing through the mist. She heard Buddy barking next to her, trying to get her attention.

She turned her dizzy head to the door of the house. It was closed. Her mother was not there. Turner was perhaps still sleeping and might not be going to school, after all. She was alone. She turned her head back towards the road. Her glasses weighed a ton. Glancing up at the bus took a ridiculous amount of time. When she finally did it was worse. All the kids were in front of her, crammed against the windows. Vivienne's mouth seemed to want to swallow her up as it opened at its full width. Her eyes did likewise. The glasses slid to the tip of her nose, and the kids burst out laughing. She clung tightly to Buddy's leash. Sensing her distress, he started howling.

Alexandra took forever to return with Turner. He was wearing a gorgeous pair of navy blue shorts with a white Polo shirt. His adorable knees protruded from the white socks with blue stripes. Vivienne's terror descended two degrees when she saw them.

"Children, we have lemonade for sale," Alexandra offered, smiling. Vivienne wished with all her might that the ground would open up at that moment and swallow her!

"Hahaha!" The kids laughed again. Alexandra turned to Vivienne. She was surprised with the behavior of the kids. *What's so funny?* she wondered.

As the bus door opened, Vivienne took a few seconds to compare herself to her mother on the reflection of the glass of the door. How different they both were. Alexandra's hair was shimmering gold and cascaded in waves at the nape of her slender neck. Hers was like the spikes of the dandelion flower; too silky and messed up with the slightest breeze. Her mother's eyes were dark and mysterious like a Greek goddess might have. Hers were light and predictable. Vivienne longed to be like her! Her mom was a work of art; polished by the most skilled artist. Meanwhile, she was the work of a novice craftsman, like her own silly drawings.

"Have a beautiful day, I love you," said Alexandra throwing a kiss into the air.

She didn't bathe them in kisses any more for it would violate one of Vivienne's important rules.

Claudia Carbonell

They were established when she turned five and attended kindergarten. By the middle of the year, she noticed that the children began to laugh at her mother's unrestrained display of affection so Vivienne forbade her to do so in public, so she stopped.

Vivienne grabbed Turner's hand and dragged herself up the bus. Her legs were heavy. It had been easier to climb Eylar Mountain than those three steps. *Oh, I sure have it coming,* she thought.

Turner seemed grouchy. She knew that Mom had awakened him all of a sudden, instead of playing the guitar and singing the song, *You are Everything and Everything is You.* Such was the way they woke up every morning. While they were getting dressed and brushed their teeth, Eric read to them pieces of biographies of important leaders. Vivienne's favorites were the memoirs of Mother Teresa and Pope Francis.

Vivienne's eyes almost crashed against her glasses, searching around for Savanah, one of her three only friends. She would impose order in a matter of seconds. The kids continued laughing and a few tried to hide it by covering their mouths. *In two more stops the bus will pick up Eva and Zenobia.* She walked to the back of the bus and, there, feeling crammed among several kids, she sat down. Turner pushed the boy at his side with his hip.

"Hey, don't push!" complained Franco, and threw a glare at Turner. Turner placed both thumbs on either side of his temples and wiggled his fingers, then proceeded to stick out his tongue at the boy.

Claudia Carbonell

Franco, in disgust, moved to a seat in front of them. The kids were still laughing.

"Now Vivienne is a lemonade seller. Hahaha!" roared Rebecca, Franco's sister. She had already promised to crush Vivienne's glasses on her face! The fact that her parents were celebrities had nothing to do with it, so she claimed; it was on account of Vivienne having four eyes.

"Serve me a glass of lemonade, Lemonade Girl, Hahaha!" thundered Lydia, another bully who thought she was superior to all based on her beauty.

"Why are you selling lemonade, Vivienne. Is it because your famous parents are becoming poor? Ha,,ha, ha!" continued Franco.

Turner began to lift his legs and crashed his feet on the metallic floor. Vivienne heard the voices as if they were inside a tube. She turned her head toward Turner. He was screaming.

The driver brutally braked. Ouch! Vivienne landed on the floor. Her landing was painful, utterly excruciating. Her knees felt like they could be broken. Turner helped to lift her up while tears streamed down his face. Vivienne's eyes burned as she struggled to stop her tears. If they welled up, the kids would crush her.

The driver sprang from his seat and lunged halfway down the bus. "Stop the noise! Are you okay?" he asked, directing his attention to Vivienne.

"Yeah," Vivienne lied while massaging her knees.

Turner was wailing.

"Why are you crying?" asked the driver.

"They're laughing at my, my..." Turner bawled.

"Don't worry, Turner, I'm fine," Vivienne insisted. "Everything is going to be all right."

"He, and she, and her," Turner said, pointing to Franco, Lydia, and Rebecca.

"Liar!" thundered Franco with his mouth exaggeratedly open.

"I haven't done a thing. I've been sitting quietly all the time," Lydia said, swinging her beautiful blond hair from side to side.

"The only disruptive kids are the Harr siblings," continued Rebecca gesturing toward Vivienne with the palm of her right hand to *just wait*.

"If there's any more racket, I'll report you all to the school principal! Do you understand?" threatened the driver.

"Understood, Mr. Chodorow." The kids said in unison. Turner covered his ears. Everyone's hypocrisy enraged him.

Turner was still crying. Vivienne grabbed his head, pulled him to her chest and whispered in his ear:

48

"Franco and Rebeca are going through a bad time and need to vent. Zenobia knows their parents' whole story. Their dad worked all his life in Mexico and saved a lot of money to come to this country to start a business and to give his kids a better education. They gave him a temporary merchant visa that would become permanent if their business succeeded. Instead, their business failed and then he was without money and without visa. That's why he asked Zenobia's mother to sponsor him to help him become legalized in this country. This situation explains their behavior."

Turner's mouth plunged wide open, for Vivienne had bombarded him with a ton of words and the only thing he understood was, *The parents of the school's worst bullies deserve to go through a bad time.*

The kids brought the volume of their laughter down a notch and, one stop later, Zenobia and Eva walked in. Both were dressed in almost identical denim skirts and purple star print blouses. They always agreed on what to wear to go to school since they enjoyed looking like twins. If only Vivienne lived closer to her three friends, she would have such a good time!

The girls surveyed the two friends from top to bottom. Judging by their reaction, they approved with the friends' clothing and they whispered their opinions as well. The boys ignored them. Vivienne wished mightily to be ignored by everyone. If she had the power of being invisible, it would be far more pleasant to go to school.

"Where is Savanah?" asked Eva

She hurried to an empty seat next to Bao, a new boy who had recently emigrated from Vietnam. Kids knew little about him since he did not speak English. Zenobia took a seat on the opposite side of where Vivienne was.

"Hi Vivienne," Zenobia said, "did you hit your knees?"

"Oh, no, did you fall again?" asked Eva turning her head to her.

"It was nothing," Vivienne assured.

"She only kneeled to kiss the floor. Ha ha," Franco bawled.

In an instant, Turner was on his feet and lunged toward Franco. "Be quiet!" He shouted and made a fist. Vivienne jumped at him and returned him to his seat. The kids roared in laughter. This time, the driver just glared via the rearview mirror. The school was just around the corner so he would have a break from the kids for eight hours.

"What's up with Turner?" asked Eva.

"He's tired," Vivienne replied.

"Leave him alone," said Zenobia glaring at Franco.

They were going around the circular driveway of the school. The first class for Vivienne was math, her worst subject.

What was most distressing of all was that there would be an exam about money. There would be plenty of additions and subtractions.

She knew how to add, but subtracting was difficult for her. It felt like a matter of life or death to pass the exam with at least a B or she risked having to go back to third grade math. Such a tragedy could not happen to her. Her parents would be so disappointed and she would be the worst example for Turner.

To be accepted to kindergarten at age four, he had to learn to tie his tennis shoes, memorize the alphabet, write his first and last name, count up to thirty, and identify all colors and shapes. He put in all this effort to attend school with Vivienne. Besides, if she was returned to third grade math, she would make her friends worry; the other twenty-two kids, well, they would pretty much destroy her.

As always, Mr. Chodorow asked the kids to line up according to height, prior to leaving the bus. Turner led the line, followed by Zenobia and Eva. Since she was the tallest, Savanah was usually the last one in line and made sure that the morons in front didn't annoy Vivienne. Unfortunately, today she was absent. Savanah commanded respect. She was a girl with strong hands and several bullies had already tasted her strength. But she was not here today.

Today, Vivienne was crammed in the middle of bullies and endured several pinches on her back, slaps on the head and one time her hair was brutally pulled. An electric shock shot up to the crown of her head.

Judging from the giggling, she knew the hair pulling had been granted by Rebecca.

Turner and his two friends waited for Vivienne on the first step of the entrance to the school. All three looked anxious.

"Are you okay, Vivienne?" asked Zenobia, examining her from head to toe.

"Yes, nothing happened," she lied. Turner fixed his gaze on her eyes with his particular suspicious stare. He was only five years old but it was impossible to fool him.

Zenobia gave her long glare to the most dangerous trio of bullies of not just fourth grade, but from the entire school: Franco, Rebecca, and Lydia.

"We must be very alert, Vivienne, since we don't have Savanah today," Zenobia warned, and they all walked to school.

A full day of challenges awaited them. As an example, while they were having breakfast, Rebecca grabbed her banana. Instead of adding it to her cereal, she pulled a black marker from her backpack and drew a face on it accented by two upward lines simulating eyes and handed it to her brother to pass it to Bao. He was an excellent target for all harassment by virtue of him being a new student, not speaking English, and being endowed with a longer face than most kids.

Franco put the fruit next to the boy's face and roared, "Question, which one is the banana and who is the new student? Right? How can you tell? Ha ha ha!"

After breakfast, the bell rang for the first class and, as always, Vivienne grabbed Turner's hand. With their friends, they raced to leave him in his kindergarten class and hurried to their classroom. They almost always arrived half to a minute late. Their teacher, Miss Hathaway, a super unpleasant redhead, took the opportunity to scold them. She couldn't understand why they did not let Turner walk to class alone.

"Vivienne's brother can walk to his class by himself," was the same roar of every morning. Savanah was the one who always responded and sometimes ended up in the principal's office. Today, Zenobia was the one who spoke for all three: "I'm sorry, Miss Hathaway, but Turner is too young to walk alone to his class." She ended with something unusual, "If he was your son, you would also take him."

Immediately, the teacher wrote a note, handed it to Zenobia, and sent her to the principal's office. Vivienne almost let a laugh escape. She turned her eyes to Eva. Her face was like a ripe tomato and her lips were also tightly sealed.

If I only had the courage to talk like Savanah and Zenobia, she thought.

Zenobia returned four minutes later with a note from the director. She handed it to the teacher and sat next to Vivienne. For Vivienne, the pleasant experiences of school were in this order:

• Going to school with Turner

• Having her three and only friends in her same classroom

• Having Zenobia as a desk partner

Miss Hathaway wasted no time in passing out the exams. "Maintain complete silence and keep your eyes on your *test*," she emphasized. "If I see anyone copying, I'll take away the exam and automatically give an F. You have fifty minutes to finish."

Vivienne checked the clock. She had forty nine minutes to complete the exam. It consisted of two written pages on both sides. There was a lot of writing and a few numbers. Those questions were the worst because it was required to understand the problems well. When she was as nervous as today, she got stunned and her mind went blank. She took a deep and slow breath, just as her dad did before a competition. She let the air out as she said to herself, *take time to read each question and answer it.*

The first one said: If you buy five pounds of flaxseeds and each pound costs seven dollars, how much do you have to pay? She imagined herself selling at her lemonade stand. There were five customers in front of her, and Turner charged them seven dollars a glass. She smiled. She could never charge so much, but, well, her brother could as a result of being so adorable. So, what she would receive would be $35.

She answered the rest of the questions by visualizing herself in her stand, selling.

Turner was always by her side and was responsible for receiving the money and keeping it in their mother's jewelry box. Vivienne was in charge of serving every glass and explaining her mission. Not once did she feel embarrassed. She spoke clearly.

She was now on the last question.

She took a deep breath and checked the clock. She had fourteen minutes left. She raised her hand. For the first time, she was the first to complete a math test before anyone else. The kids were surprised. Eva and Zenobia smiled at her and made the best gesture of approval: two thumbs up.

"Zenobia and Eva," the teacher warned, "stay focused on the exam."

Uff, Vivienne thought, *she always ruins a pleasant moment for me.*

"You, Vivienne, can go out for a while. Come back in ten minutes, understood?" She nodded and hurried towards the koi pond. Surrounded by pink currants, it was the most beautiful place in school.

The pleasant moments at school, aside from sharing time with Turner and her friends, were few. She sat on the edge of the pool and dropped her gaze to the fish. The happiest moment of her life was when Turner was born.

The memory of Turner's birth was worth remembering in every detail. Since her earliest recollection, she had begun to beg her parents to buy a baby. This happened when she was just three years old. Months later, her mother acquired a formidable belly. Inside her was the most anticipated being from heaven in the entire world, her brother.

Two months before she turned four, her dad rushed to her crying and uttering the most wonderful words she had ever heard: "Princess, your little brother will be born today."

Yet, when he added the rest, he spoiled her magical moment: "I must be with your mom. Wait until the baby is born. Be patient, all right?"

No, how could she patiently wait while the most extraordinary event in history was taking place? She was dumbstruck.

Her mother was in the room and she could not go in. She spent the whole day walking from one end to the other end of the long hallway on the second floor. She walked miles and miles, memorizing every line and crack of that long wooden floorboard. She never walked so much. Not even when she hiked the Eylar Mountain with her dad or in Knotts Berry Farm. Her feet were burning.

How much she yearned to storm right through that door and be there to witness the most beautiful miracle of all. It was not possible, she had to wait. It was 11:15 in the morning, on Wednesday, October 15, 2010, a school day.

She was dressed and her hair was impeccably combed with the diamond headband that her mom had bought at a local handicraft show.

She was wearing her favorite pink Barbie sandals and a pink organza dress that she only wore for very special occasions, such as Savanah's birthday. The birth of her brother merited to be dressed in her most elegant clothing and to stay home.

It was the only day she missed school without being sick. Her parents understood. Hearing the baby's feeble cry made her heart overflow with a deep and inexplicable love. She threw herself at the door and slammed it with both fists. She had to be the first one to carry him, to lull him, and kiss him. The midwife opened the door. A light blue-and-white striped bundle was resting on Alexandra's chest. She had watery eyes. Eric was crying and holding her hand. Vivienne flew to the bedside. On her knees, she leaned towards him.

"I want to check every part of him!" she demanded.

Alexandra laid him on the bed and Vivienne began to unwrap him. His face was tiny as well as his nose and mouth. His arms were too thin and his hands were clenched. He threw fists into the air, proving what he would be like when he grew up. Once he was unsaddled, Vivienne uttered a shriek and almost fainted, and rightly so.

Her little brother had a long navel that was pressed by a hook to dry clothes. Her parents spent a long time to comfort her.

Once she understood that the baby had been fed with their mom's nutrients for nine months through that umbilical cord attached to Alexandra's stomach, she stopped wailing. She proceeded counting his toes and fingers. She wrapped her brother, kissed his feet, forehead, head, and lay down next to him. Turner then opened a hand and squeezed Vivienne's index finger. *Since then, we never let go,* she thought.

Giggles coming from behind her erased the image. It was Rebecca, Franco, and Lydia. Their expressions showed sarcasm. Rebecca's face had written all over the desire to tear her apart. Vivienne's eyes almost crashed against her glasses. She jumped and raced away. She knew at best she would end up inside the pool and, very likely, with a fish inside her mouth if she didn't instantly vanish.

A hand that felt as thick and heavy as a brown bear claw took her by the neck, tossed her to the floor, and two bricks landed on her belly. They were two knees. Her glasses flew afar. Everything went cloudy. They pulled her hair and a torrential of smacks landed on her arms, hips, and head, especially on her face. The bell rang. She felt relief when the group of culprits scampered away.

"What do you get by hitting me? Aah! Aah!" She shouted. She felt around, searching for her glasses. *Good Lord, I hope they left them,* she thought.

They were resting on her chest and, fortunately, they were intact. She fixed her hair and clothes, then hurried back to her class. As soon as she walked in, Miss Hathaway's kitchen clock chimed. The kids all jumped out of their seats.

Judging by the protests, many were unable to finish answering all questions. Fortunately, Zenobia and Eva were calm. They both looked at each other and smiled as they returned to their desks.

All day long, Vivienne thought about the beating she endured and about Bao's mockery. This boy had probably left loved ones in his country of origin in exchange for another one. Most likely, he came to the U.S. in search of a promising future through equality, freedom, financial comfort, and the right to be happy, which constitute the *"American Dream."* She had the option to complain to the school principal, however, the consequences would've been worse. The tattletales were double bullied.

She just had to concentrate on her mission of selling lemonade to free kids who were less fortunate than her. During recess she talked about her stand with her friends. Turner listened enthusiastically and gave a splendid idea of adding a piece of different fruit to each glass. Vivienne gladly accepted the idea as long as he was the one cutting the fruit with a butter knife. Turner then realized that the lemonade with the agreed recipe was more appetizing.

"Vivienne, I want to see your stand!" said Zenobia enthusiastically.

"Oh, I'll go everyday to help you sell," Eva promised.

By the end of the school day, the kids, including the bullies, were tired and overwhelmed by their exams. At Pleasantville Elementary School, all the teachers agreed to give exams the same day. So much of the bullies' energy, especially their neurons was spent on thinking. Consequently, they lost interest in harassing others.

When Vivienne got home, she did her homework with Turner in the tree house and she served cereal for them. Once they finished, she and Turner hurried after Eric who was taking the stand outside. Alexandra had the lemonade ready in the fridge.

"Thanks, Mommy!" said Vivienne with a wide smile and took the jar.

"Wait, my dear, I'll carry it for you," her mother offered, and grabbed the pitcher.

Once again, the stand was open for its mission at the end of Harmony Street. Vivienne felt a great sense of joy. The forest was behind her. She was listening to the flow of the stream and the orchestra of thousands of birds. Her beloved family stood in front of her stand, while she dreamed of making a lot of sales for an awesome cause.

"Princess," her dad said, "you are setting out on a very hard mission." She studied his face. It showed anxiety. She read it in the pursing of his lips and in his deep frown. "Think about it, Vivienne." *Now he's insanely worried,* she thought. *Whenever he refers to me by my name, it is sign that he is really freaking out.*

"Let me explain myself," he continued. "By you just showing compassion for the child slaves in the photo, you have shown that you have the greatest heart I have ever known.

"Most people only care about their own lives. While you, beloved, by just thinking of helping those forgotten children, you have shown your true beauty. You have nothing more to prove."

"Dad," she wailed, feeling the blood leap to her face, "I don't want to prove anything. I want to help. You said it, those children are forgotten."

Alexandra approached them with the jug of lemonade. She placed it on top of the stand and intervened, "But precious, you are only a child." She had obviously listened to the conversation. "As much as you want, how much could you do for them?"

Vivienne would have preferred that the school bullying continue all day than seeing her mother's face show pity for her.

"Momma," she responded, struggling to hold back her tears, "I'm going to free them. I will, I will," she insisted, stamping the floor with one foot.

"But, my child," continued Eric, "don't forget; you're just a little girl." He touched the tip of her nose. "We always impose limits upon ourselves, yet we must recognize that we do have them."

"Dad, you once read me a quotation from Ghandi that says, *if we can dream it, we can achieve it.*"

Certainly, Eric had once read the aforementioned quote. As a motivator, he enjoyed reading to his family the greatest teachings of world's leaders.

Eric took her hand and kissed it. "Are you sure about this?"

"Yes, Daddy."

"It will be difficult, very difficult. Besides, you can not neglect your studies. Remember, school comes first."

"I know," she replied. "I'll do all my homework and then I'll come out to sell lemonade."

"Well then, I respect your decision. Love, what do you think?" he asked turning to Alexandra.

"I support you, my baby, in every way. But don't forget, you're just a little girl."

"I don't understand you guys. You both said that slavery is very sad."

"True, it is. It's also unfair," Alexandra agreed. Eric nodded approvingly.

They went silent. Vivienne's gaze was as firm as the day she asked for a little sister. Alexandra nodded. Eric took her hand.

"We'll be at home," Eric said. "But as soon as you get tired, Princess, come home. Agree?"

"All right," she answered. She felt disgusted by her age. If she were a teenager it would not be a big deal to do what she wanted to accomplish.

It was five in the afternoon. Time for their favorite show, *Super Galaxy*. She always watched it with Turner. Today, she was sitting in front of the stand with a huge pitcher of lemonade on a desolate street. Behind her, the forest rocked with animals, beautiful landscapes, and secret places that only she, her brother, and her friends, knew. But from now on, until she raised the necessary funds to free the child slaves in the world, she could not return to her magical place. She would devote all of her time to her stand.

Turner, sitting on the sidewalk, was throwing stones on the road. He was dangerously bored. Vivienne saw it in the way he wiggled his arms, lifted his shoulders, and kicked the air.

"Turner, you seem tired. If you want, go home," she suggested.

"Are we both going in?" he asked hopefully.

"No, I must stay," she replied. She felt tired of waiting. It had only been three hours since they had come home from school, and it seemed like thousands of hours. She sat next to her brother. He cradled his chin in one hand and rested his arm on his thigh. He looked dispirited.

"Seriously Turner, go home and watch *Super Galaxy*."

"I said no, that's a dumb show!"

It was not. Besides, it was the only TV program their parents allowed them to watch. Their schedule was too busy with gym classes and swimming practice to watch more than one TV show a day.

"It's not true, Turner. You love that show!"

"I no longer like it!" he insisted and plunged him in behind the stand.

It was awesome to have a partner for everything. They attended sports practice together; they were going to the same school; and they were now working to make her dream come true. Although he did not understand it completely, he shared it with her. He did it out of love for her. He also put all his efforts to learn a world of new things to be able to go to school with her.

It would have been easier and much more fun for him to stay home watching TV much of the day like most four-year-olds, but for Turner to be with his sister was more important than having fun. Her heart doubled in size, and so she stood up.

"Wait for me Turner, I'll be right back," she said, and hurried home.

"Are you guys coming in?" Alexandra asked hopefully. She was by the window watching them.

"No, Mommy, we haven't sold a single glass yet," Vivienne replied breathlessly. "I came in to pick up my backpack." She ran to her room, took her heavy bag where she had all her schoolbooks and stuffed it with other ones. It was so crammed up she couldn't zip it up. She placed it on her back and tightened the straps on her chest. Hunching over, she left the room. Her father was about to walk into her bedroom to find out what was going on.

"What are you doing with that backpack so loaded with books, Princess? Let me help you," he insisted, grabbing the straps.

"I'm fine, Dad. I don't need help," she affirmed walking down the stairs while gripping tightly onto the hand rail.

"Do you have more homework?" he asked, following her.

As she opened the door she said, "There's no one on the street today.

It's been three hours and we've sold nothing, Turner is very tired, and if I carry this heavy backpack, I'll remind myself why I'm making this effort."

Alexandra stuck her head out from behind the back of the sofa. From there, she was now watching over Turner. She turned to Eric and said, "You hear that, Eric?"

"Doll, you're going to hurt your back," he insisted. "Let Daddy carry your books."

"I'll be fine, really. Don't worry about me."

The next day, fortunately Savanah had recovered from an episode of asthma which allowed her to retake the role of Vivienne's bodyguard. As soon as Vivienne and Turner left for school, Eric and Alexandra went out to distribute flyers throughout the neighborhood. They were professionally written by Eric. They read:

Dear Neighbors:

We ask you to support our 9-year-old daughter, Vivienne Harr, who is selling lemonade for a beautiful cause: to end child slavery. Her stand of delicious and nutritious lemonade (without preservatives or refined sugar) awaits at the end of Harmony Street. Thank you for your support☺

It did not matter that Lydia, who lived one street over to hers, was one of the neighbors who got the flyer.

Phew, I know what awaits me, Vivienne thought, *I must always remain next to Savanah.*

For two consecutive days, Zenobia, Eva, and Savanah accompanied Vivienne and Turner at the stand. It was fun to do homework together, tell stories, read tales, and sell a couple of glasses of lemonade to neighbors. At 7 p.m., the stand was lifted and taken inside the house.

Eric measured the remaining lemonade and bought it for the family. Vivienne was sad since she wanted to sell it to other people. She yearned to make her cause known and be supported by all of Pleasanton.

At school, the mockery toward her increased. Now they called her the lemonade seller. The bullies had more reasons than ever to tease her.

On the bus, the bathroom, the playground, and even in the classroom in front of Ms. Hathaway, the bullies began, "Did you know that Miss Magu wants to free the slaves of the world?"

"Who does she think she is?..."

"Abraham Lincoln..."

"Mother Teresa?…"

"Martin Luther King?"

Savanah was in constant battle answering to every offense and Turner was always vigilant to defend his sister. The terrible thing was that while the intimidators harassed, the others laughed. Miss Hathaway was more prudent but Vivienne knew she also thought that her idea was ridiculous.

Even her friends reminded her of how impossible her dream was. A little girl had never changed the world in such a way. They only accompanied her at the stand for two more days. Thereafter, they even avoided talking about the stand. It had become an old story. *Fortunately, the school year is about to end,* Vivienne forced this thought frequently to calm down.

Amidst grievances, bullying, hair pulling, and long hours at her stand with a jar of lemonade in front of an empty street, finally, June 2 arrived; the last day of school.

Miss Hathaway asked every student to come to the front of the class to answer the following question: "What will you do during the holidays?"

Roland would spend it with his dad's side of the family in Seville, Spain.

Lydia was going to the Bahamas.

Savanah and her parents would visit Greece, a country she always dreamed of visiting. An admirer of Greek mythology like her had to spend some time savoring the country from where so many beautiful legends had originated.

Of all, Savanah was the most applauded. She spoke eloquently and was convincing. Her voice was as strong as her character. It did not bother her at all to be endowed with a big body. Even when she just started school last year, the bullies stared at her and commented on her weight. She put her hands on her hips and shouted at them, "The mirror shows my body every day, and I'm fine with it! If any of you are not, we can discuss it outside." Strangely, no one else commented on the matter. Even Lydia insisted that she was a growing girl and did not know why a few considered her overweight.

With a broad smile, Eva said that her parents would take her to Knotts Berry Farm.

Zenobia would visit her grandparents in Chicago.

The rest of the students passed to the front of the class. The last one was Vivienne. All eyes were focused on her. Lydia folded her arms and rested her face on them ready to hide her face for she knew she would burst in laughter. Franco stepped aside to have a better view of her.

Once in front of the class, Vivienne lowered her head, raised her glasses with the tip of her forefinger, and whispered, "I'll stay home selling lemonade."

That was the funniest joke in the world. The whole class burst out laughing. Her friends covered their mouths and stared at each other in disbelief.

What kind of strange bug had stung her? Why didn't she come up with a pious lie instead of exposing herself to greater mockery from everyone?

"Attention kids!" the teacher yelled. All had lost the auditory faculty and raised the skill of laughter. Some held their bellies with both hands fearing they would explode.

"Order, I say!" Ms. Hathaway insisted. They calmed down as soon as she threatened to bring in the principal. His name brought out the best behavior even from the worst bullies.

Vivienne kept her head down and returned to her desk. She kept this position during the bus ride back home. On two occasions, the driver had to stop the bus to impose order. Since it was the last day of school and there were no consequences for their bad behavior, the kids continued to tease her until the bus stopped in front of her house. Turner cried all the way home.

"Don't worry," Vivienne insisted. "It's going to be all right."

The truth was that for Turner, everything got worse since now his sister took out the stand in the morning after breakfast and brought it back home late at night. This was repeated day after day, even on weekends. Talk about the worst vacations ever! She refused to go to the beach, to the movies, to restaurants, to the tree house, and to the forest. When she got tired from lack of sales, she hung her heavy school bag on her back to remind her of the weight the two slave children in the photo were carrying.

She had become boring and only talked about freeing the kid slaves worldwide. *What horrible vacations I'm having!* Turner thought.

Sales were less promising. On good days, they sold twenty dollars. On bad ones, they only sold two. Vivienne made an estimate. The average sales were eight to twelve dollars a day. At that rate it would take her 18,750 days or 51 years to accumulate the $150,000. She would get old in front of the stand. She would most likely be married and also perhaps be a grandma by then.

Three weeks after school vacation, the annual Summer Fair opened in Pleasanton. Apart from Knotts Berry Farm, it was perhaps the happiest place on earth. In it, there were a world of attractions, such as race cars, a Ferris wheel, a carousel, a gigantic trampoline, and the most varied food and ice cream in one place.

"Guess where we are going today, kids?" Alexandra asked while smiling. Turner opened his eyes wide. Vivienne knew what it was about. She had seen the ad in the newspaper.

"You guys go with Turner to the fair. I'll stay."

Alexandra paled and faced Eric.

"We have to do something!"

"I agree. She's serious," Eric agreed. Turning to Vivienne, said, "Princess, I never thought you'd go this far. Okay, I'll take you as my client.

Every day, I will film you and you will have to write a note in all media, such as Twitter, Facebook, and Medium. You will do this for 365 consecutive days. Agree?"

"Yes Daddy!" Vivienne roared and threw her arms around him.

"You started in the summer. It's the beginning of fall and the weather is about to change. It will get cold; it will rain. You will get very tired. Are you sure you're going to resist so much?"

"Yes, I promise."

She strolled around the circular dead-end street near her house. Her backpack was so heavy! She remembered the photo of the museum. She thought, *Nobody understands why I'm so interested in you. I do not understand it myself. Possibly because I know what it feels like to be despised by the kids at school. It may be the way you feel, only a lot worse since you don't have freedom, and perhaps you don't even have a family.*

She couldn't see Turner in the stand. But as she got closer, she found him sleeping with his head nestled in his arms. His eyelashes were wet. He cried because he didn't go to the fair. It was all her fault. *My poor angel. I should not subject him to this,* she thought. She sat next to him and pulled out a book. It would be a long day.

Claudia Carbonell

Aatish and Ballabh didn't say goodbye to their grandmother due to their mom's insistence that she should sleep. Inside their tent, the boys had almost their entire wardrobe, which was all in pairs: their blue jeans, shirts, sandals, and Grandfather's apparel: two pairs of trench trousers that Grandma had sewn by hand, a wool sweater, three old torn shirts, and two pairs of shoes.

They were both wearing Dad's only pants, and the two shirts he had worn the most. The accident that had taken his life was a subject that was not discussed and the brain refused to recreate. His death had taught the villagers about the meaning of irony. Aarau Singh had been a nomad all his life, but as soon as he sat foot on Gahate, he was fascinated by its surroundings.

On the western side amidst a nest of rocks, a waterfall emanated and bathed the lower terraces of the village. A waterfall poured out and formed a stream that meandered from end to end on the peak of the mountain and reached the east where it cascaded down to the Indrawati River.

The boys' grandmother begged her son to settle there. They would have everything for their sustenance in one place. They had water. Hens would provide them with eggs, and goats and cows with milk. They bought an old house from a villager. It was a battered barn. The rain and the strong winds tore out pieces of shingles and sent them to the ground.

Aarau climbed to the roof every day to repair it. By the third week, he was just finishing when his foot slipped on the residue of a Himalayan red-tailed monal and he fell to his death. His blood ran through the grout in between the rocks and drained in the flowing stream. Thus, the villagers said that the Indrawati River was bathed with Aarau's blood.

Mom bundled up something and as the boys boarded the truck, she tucked it inside the tent wrapper. Once the brothers settled down with the other twelve kids, they began to bawl their goodbyes to their families.

Karishma was shaking up and howling. Of all, she was the one who cried most loudly. Of the children, Aatish and Ballabh were those who begged the most to stay in the village.

"Why is Granny not coming out to say goodbye?" Aatish protested.

"Tell Granny I love her!" Ballabh insisted.

"Come back soon, my little ones!" Karishma pleaded.

She approached the driver's window, bowing and imploring to the gentleman Devang to take care of her little angels.

The truck shuffled forward. The kids who were standing fell to the metal floor of the vehicle. They sat on it and rubbed their knees. Those who didn't fall hugged each other. Ballabh opened the tent and unrolled the wrapper his mother had slid inside. It was Grandma's wool scarf and her handkerchief. It was freshly washed and still wet, yet it was still stained with their grandmother's discolored blood.

The long hours wove into days, then the days were chained into weeks, and suddenly the leaves of the Catalpa trees carpeted the front of Vivienne's house, announcing that summer was over. A new school year was beginning. Vivienne was about to enter fifth grade. For 67 days, her dad had filmed her at her stand.

She was there when she was happy and at other times she felt discouraged to go out to the empty street. She knew the neighbors on one or two occasions had bought lemonade and would not buy more. Eric filmed her when she would have preferred to be playing with Turner in the forest and those three days when Buddy was recovering from an operation on his front left leg as a result of a splinter that got inserted when he was strolling with Eric and Turner in the forest.

Two days before going back to school, Channel 4 News called to interview Vivienne.

The first day of school, Vivienne and Turner picked up their backpacks from the fence of their house while Alexandra was taking the lemonade jug back home.

Just then, the news truck, followed by the school bus, reached the dead end street called Harmony, and stood in front of the last house surrounded by Catalpas, the residence of Vivienne Harr. The girl with the lemonade stand who wanted to free the child slaves around the world.

The kids were crammed into the windows facing Vivienne's house. Their eyes popped at the sight of the well-known journalist, Ann Curry. She was getting out of the vehicle holding a microphone. A big man followed her carrying a camera. Ann Curry stood in front of the cameraman and started interviewing Vivienne.

Ann Curry: "Are you Vivienne Harr?"

"Yes," she answered, raising her gaze to the bus.

The kids dropped their jaws. Eva and Zenobia had spent the night at Savanah's house, so all three were together. They were the only ones who seemed pleased.

"Now, let's see, how does it feel to see Vivienne of all people, being interviewed by the most important newscast of the country?" Savanah shouted. The question, of course, was directed mainly to Franco, Rebecca, and Lydia. During the holidays, they had carefully planned a whole list of jokes and mischief to execute on Vivienne.

To their misfortune, everyone could hear Ann Curry's questions.

"Vivienne, for 67 days you have been in front of this stand, selling lemonade for this cause: freeing child slaves of the world. What motivated you to do it?"

The interview took seven minutes. Mr. Chodorow didn't bother the wait and kept his eyes locked on the reporter the whole time. She hurried into the bus and asked, "Who are Vivienne's friends?"

Everyone raised their hands while shouting:

"Me!"

"Me!"

"Me!"

"Me!"

Vivienne said, "My three best friends are Zenobia, Eva, and Savanah, and here they are," she emphasized pointing at them. They were sitting on the last row of seats of the bus. They were saving two chairs for her and Turner. "They are the best friends in the world," she added with a smile.

They burst into nervous giggles.

"Girls, do you think your friend will achieve her dream of freeing eighteen million child slaves?" Ann inquired as she walked toward them.

Savanah was the first to answer, "If anyone can do something impossible, it's Vivienne."

"It will be difficult," Eva agreed, "but I think she will."

"I think so too, plus she'll have our support," affirmed Zenobia.

"And who is this handsome boy?" Ann asked turning to Turner. He was hiding his face behind Vivienne's back. The microphone felt threatening to him. Besides, he didn't care to talk in front of the morons in the bus.

"He's my brother, Turner. He's my greatest supporters and one of my biggest heroes."

Turner lowered his head and pressed his forehead hard against his sister's back. He felt so ashamed. Sisters shouldn't express themselves so highly of their brothers, especially when they were younger than them.

"One day, we will talk, Turner. For now, I wish both of you the best in your endeavors," said the reporter as she walked down the bus aisle, thanking Mr. Chodorow.

That day, the kids lined up to walk into the fifth grade classroom, located at the end of the hallway on the second floor. Savannah dropped her guard since she knew that the bullies won't be teasing Vivienne. Even a child with an inferior level of intelligence has a high understanding of popularity, which is to be accepted and respected by a large number of people.

To seek that approval, they get close to those who have attained it in hopes to grab some attention.

Miss Hathaway had been promoted to fifth grade, and a new teacher would be in charge of fourth grade. Every student stepped in front of the class to talk about what they had done during the holidays.

Everyone had a lot of fun, all except Vivienne. She had spent the summer working. However, this time, she was the one who was most applauded. Her having been interviewed by the famous reporter became the most talked about subject at school. Now, every child wanted to be by her side.

Every day, Vivienne's desire to raise the $150,000 escalated to an obsession. She saw this number everywhere and her brain automatically converted the numbers one, zero, and five towards her sales goal. Eric contacted the No Profit Foundation, and all money generated from sales of the lemonade was sent to them.

Now, every time someone came up to ask how much the glass of lemonade cost, Vivienne answered: "Pay whatever your heart tells you," as she showed the picture that taught her about child slavery. One time a man pulled out the last penny of his wallet which amounted to $122!

The weather was seriously freezing. The worst days were when it rained or when Pleasanton was hit by strong winds.

Eight times, the winds were so severe that Eric had to run to the stand to hold it with his considerable strength so that it would not fly away. On those days, nobody left their homes to buy lemonade. The forest behind Harmony Street roared and several trees collapsed. Still, Vivienne stood in front of her stand.

The change of weather and the continuous exposure to the freezing temperature for long hours caused Vivienne to catch a bad cold. On September 12, 2011, she began to feel a headache and pain in her bones, and ended with sneezing, watery eyes, and a high fever.

"I must be at my stand!" she demanded in response to her parents' insistence that she stay in. Her health came first. She cried and raised the volume of her begging to her parents to let her work. It was not to be. Mom and Dad were determined to keep her inside.

Vivienne came up with an idea: she installed a big sign at the end of the street which read: *Lemonade for sale at House # 3 on Harmony Street·* Next to the door of the house, Eric sat the stand. Vivienne watched all the activity outside through the front window: NONE! She was wrapped in a thick blanket, with a box of tissues at her side, with Turner eager to serve each glass. However, that day there was not a single sale.

The following day, her fever had gone down but a severe sore throat and joint pain lingered. She pretended to feel great and brought out her stand.

She followed suit during Christmas and the New Year. Seven months had passed: 210 days, and sales amounted to $5,210. Her parents had contributed $3,000 to the total sales.

The low number of sales did nothing to truncate the avalanche of publicity that Vivienne was generating.

Eric was struggling to keep up with the demands of the media. In the evenings, after returning the stand to the house, he took Vivienne to interviews. Most radio stations were several hours away. They decided to take the kids out of school and educate them at home. Alexandra would be the new teacher.

Savanah, Zenobia, and Eva jumped at the opportunity to take classes at the Harr residence. Their parents were delighted. Of everyone, Turner was the most excited to spend all day with his sister and her friends. Besides, having Buddy cuddled at their feet was so much fun. The best part of all was that there were no bullies to worry about.☺

One Friday, Vivienne sent a Tweet with the following message:

Today at the end of Harmony Street in Pleasanton, California, there will be lemonade, despite the rain.

New York Times writer Nicholas Kristof replied with:

Since I'm in New York, regretfully I'm not able to go.

Eric was in charge of checking Vivienne's messages when he stumbled on Nicholas's Tweet. He asked Vivienne, "Baby, have you seen the message Nicholas Kristof sent you?"

"Yes, Dad but I don't know him."

"Well, I do! He's the famous New York Times journalist and author of *The Center of Heaven.*"

"Dad, later today we must go to the book store to buy his book" she replied immediately. Then she wrote the following to Nicholas:

Thanks, Nicholas. Today I will go to the bookstore to buy your book.

Nicholas replied:

I will soon fly to California to try the lemonade of the girl who wants to free the child slaves around the world.

Then the magic of the media was summoned when this exchange of messages was seen by thousands of people and went viral. Thousands of readers answered the last message from the famous writer, eager to support a girl with a great dream.

An avalanche of journalists called the Harr residence every day anxious to interview Vivienne, including Jeff Probst of the famous show which bears his name. For the interview, she had to travel to Hollywood. They all went, including Buddy. The studio where the program was filmed was dark and divided by movable walls made of thin metal sheet.

As soon as Buddy barged in, he took the grip of his leash between his teeth. He pulled it from Vivienne's hands and went mad with the noise, the cameras, the mess in the makeup room, and the number of people coming and going. Logically, he had to impose order! He raced left to right, up and down.

Vivienne, Turner and their parents ran after him shouting, "Stop, Buddy, do not run!"

We know little of the canine dialect and the auditory mechanism of dogs. Somehow, it is likely that they tend to understand the messages the other way around.

The Harr family was shouting, "Stop!" But he seemed to be hearing, "Make as much trouble as possible and tear down the walls." That was exactly what Buddy did every time his family approached him to take away the leash between his teeth.

Jeff Probst was in the makeup room when one of the walls landed on his knees. With a laugh, he said, "I imagine this particular visitor is a member of the Harr family!"

Buddy sat up and put a paw on the wall which moments before had divided the makeup room.

"The pleasure is mine," Jeff said.

"Buddy, oh, how embarrassing!" Vivienne, shouted, blushing, an action followed by Turner.

"Sorry, it's our dog," she explained, lowering her pet's paw from the lap of the one who was about to interview her on TV.

Alexandra and Eric came in. They apologized and laughed. Once Buddy had made sure that all the disorder was just atmospheric and that people were trustworthy, he behaved like a gentleman. When the assistants re-erected the walls, he didn't even sniff them.

Eric had warned Vivienne that the first televised interview was always the hardest. In a studio surrounded by hundreds of people, lights, and cameras, the show began.

"Today we have a nine-year-old girl who has been in front of her house for 90 days, at a stand built by her father, selling lemonade. You will think, what's new about a girl selling lemonade outside her home? Many kids do. What's different about our guest today is her mission. She does not take a penny from sales. She collects all the funds to free child slaves around the world. You heard right, ladies and gentlemen: her purpose is to liberate eighteen million child slaves.

Here we have her. Give a loud applause to the girl who is making history: Vivienne Harr!"

A black curtain divided a narrow space where the makeup artist was applying the last touches of loose powder to Vivienne's face and the assistant was giving the last words of encouragement: "Everything will be fine," she said.

"Princess, are you ready?" her dad asked.

"Remember, it's all about the heart," Mom insisted.

Turner was holding tightly on Buddy's leash while he was trying to break loose anew.

The ground began to swell. She felt dizzy and a high-pitched whistle blew in her ears: *As soon as you walk through the black curtain, you will face death.*

"Feeling good, my love?" Eric asked as Alexandra massaged her shoulders.

She remembered that they had traveled from far away with the whole family. Her dad had stopped working with his clients to devote all his time to her. Turner had always been at her side on the stand, even when he was bored to death. Her mother helped her prepare the lemonade and gave her so much support with her immense love. She did not have any other choice but to answer all the questions *perfectly.* She could not be ... well, her.

She had to become a different girl. One filled with self confidence, sense of humor, coherence, and brilliance.

"You are all that and more," her parents reassured. She didn't know if she thought of those attributes or she said them out loud and her parents answered her, or simply they had read her mind. They were so extraordinary that it would not be strange if they had prophetic powers. "Princess, breathe slowly and deeply," her father advised. Just then, the host said, "I don't know what happened to our guest today ... Vivienne, are you here?"

Turner giggled nervously and Buddy squealed, watching her with empathetic eyes. She took a deep breath, placed her fingers in the opening of the curtain and pushed it aside.

She walked out in front of an audience. They were live. Live!

"Ground, swallow me!" She whispered and exhaled.

Trying as best she could to balance her walk around the bulging floor, she dragged herself endlessly until she was in front of Jeff. He had risen to his feet.

"Welcome, welcome. Vivienne Harr, ladies and gentlemen!" The audience whistled and applauded. However, she was beginning to lack air.

She saw herself standing in front of her classroom while the kids roared all kinds of hurtful comments and Miss Hathaway crushed her with her reproving glance. After class, if Savanah was not watching her, the bullies dropped on top of her.

"Vivienne," Jeff began. "We know about your mission. Now, we want to know why you are interested on slaves. Why not animal cruelty? The environment? Climate change?"

Now, she saw herself standing in front of the picture of those two children carrying the heavy rocks on their backs. "All the problems that affect the world also touch me," she responded and gazed up at the wall in front of her. There was a huge screen recording her face. Each of her words was being heard by more than three hundred million people in the fifty states of the United States. Among them were the school bullies of her school and in all the public schools in the country. On the other hand, there were the children in the picture who represented those eighteen million slaves whom she had promised to free.

She took another deep breath and talked about her visit to the museum with her dad. For once, she ignored the cameras and the television screen in front of her. She felt comfortable with Jeff. She was staring at his face. He smiled at her all the time and reassured her of how important her mission was.

"Vivienne, if you could send a message to the child slaves of the world, what would it be?"

"I want them to know that everything's going to be all right; that soon life will change for them."

"What do you want most in life?"

"To free all the slaves in the world while I'm alive."

The audience stood up and applauded. Vivienne turned to look around. Most people were crying. Everyone was shouting her name. Even when Jeff said goodbye to her and she disappeared behind the curtain, people were still madly shouting her name and were clapping.

She would always remember that day.

A whole film crew soon followed the the Catalpa trees had turned yellow and fell like a flood Harr family for nine months, documenting their lives. Once again, the Catalpa flowers carpeted the front of their house.

By the time the filmmakers were satisfied with what they had captured on camera, the leaves of of golden hearts. By then, it was December 12, 2012. According to the Mayan calendar, on this day the world would end.

It was the best time to bring the lemonade stand to New York Times Square, to better spread the message of Vivienne's mission of freedom to more than ninety thousand attendees.

A reporter approached the family and asked, "If today was the end of the world, what would you like to be doing?" They all looked at each other, and Vivienne replied, "Exactly this!"

A lightning bolt caught the attention of the people. All eyes glanced up at the sky, and a shower of cotton flecks dropped down. People grabbed their hands and began to sing Eddie James' song entitled, *Freedom*. People raised their voice in an exciting yell when they got to the part that said,

No more shackles,

no more chains,

no more bondage,

I am free!

Soon, the street and the heads of the attendees were covered with snow. It seemed as if Vivienne was offering hot chocolate instead of ice-cold lemonade.

Everyone wanted to be part of the movement she had created.

At the end of the night, the Peninsula Hotel sent the Harr family lemonade with hot ginger on a silver platter. At midnight, people shouted: "We are still alive! We are alive!" Life continued, and Vivienne had reached her goal: $150,000 in sales.

Eric, with tearful eyes, approached her and said, "Princess, you did it at last; you've reached your goal."

Turner hugged her and Alexandra pinched her cheeks. "How do you feel after raising so much money?"

"Are we done with slavery?" Vivienne asked.

Eric and Alexandra sat eyes on one another in surprise. Vivienne watched them closely and Turner, pulling out his mom's cashmere sweater, begged, "Please say yes, just say YES!"

One of the reporters was recording the family and brought the camera to Eric's face.

"No, slavery is not over," he answered.

"Then my work is not over either," replied Vivienne.

During the flight home, Vivienne did not cease to propose different ways to earn more money for the liberation of slaves. Now she wanted not only to free children but also adults.

The total number of slaves in the world amounted to 30 million.

"No one deserves to be mistreated in such a way and to work so much just to benefit a greedy man!" she protested to her parents.

"Sweetheart, you're right, but how can we possibly raise more money? Our bank account now shows that we are poor. This happened because we have taken out a lot more money than what your mom and I were able to deposit."

"There should be a way to do it. I just know it," insisted Vivienne.

The day Vivienne announced her brilliant idea to soon free the thirty million slaves of the world, their bank account had reached a negative balance. She proposed to pack the lemonade in bottles just like Coca-Cola or Pepsi. Crazily enough, her parents again, accepted her idea. This time they would use plastic money, conveniently called *credit cards.*

Vivienne had never liked subtraction and even less in those days when she understood her parents' financial dilemma. They owed money to the bank. This was a result of having mortgaged the house, invested all their savings in thousands of bottles and raw materials for the preparation of lemonade, and making marketing efforts, without any results.

The sum total of all anguish fell on Eric and Alexandra the day the bank started calling to remind them to begin paying the mortgage. If not, the beautiful house at the end of Harmony Street at the back of one of the most magical forests in California, surrounded by Catalpas, with apple trees crowned with the kids' tree house, would be owned by the bank.

That day, the bank sent the Harr family an *official* letter. This time their financial institution was no longer threatening them but was taking legal action.

"Vivienne, we can't go on. Forgive us little one, but we are about to lose our house!" Alexandra begged. She had opened the envelope from the bank that stipulated the value of the house after the mortgage. The Harr owed more money than the house was worth. Although for them, the true value was in the memories that were framed in those walls.

"No, Mommy," Vivienne cried. "We can't give up!"

Eric listened to Vivienne crying and ran to her, followed by Buddy. "What's going on?" he asked. Buddy was already standing on his hind legs and had placed his forelegs on Vivienne's shoulders so he could lick her tears. "Uuf!" he begged her to stop crying, but she was inconsolable.

"Look at this letter from the bank, Eric," Alexandra shrieked, passing it to him. The sides of her mouth were drooping.

"Oh no! The bank is about to take the house from us." Turning to Vivienne, he said, "Princess, we must first attend to our affairs before we take on the problems of the world."

"Daddy, if it's not us, who will take care of them?" she protested raising the volume of her weeping. Buddy yelped and kept on with his duty of licking her tears. Holding onto the very walls she might soon beyond reach of touching, Vivienne arrived at the sofa in the living room.

She laid down and cried. Turner sat down next to her, took her head and laid it on his thighs. "It's going to be all right," he whispered, holding back his own tears so he would not hurt her further. Buddy sat next to her, put his snout on her chest, and fixed his eyes on hers, ready to lick her tears away.

Where do your dreams end up when you no longer have the resources to nourish them? thought Vivienne. They were as fragile as a child. They needed food and a healthy environment to grow. But the slave kids did not enjoy any of them.

The picture of those two kids from the museum materialized again in her head. Instead of a static snapshot, now it moved. The boys flexed their knees as if they were determined to jump off the cliff. Before they did, she raised her legs up high.

"Excuse me, Buddy," she ordered. The dog got up and barked. She stamped her feet on the ground and shook off the dizziness she had and once the floor was immediately flattened, she ran to her parents.

"Dad, Mom," she shouted, looking over her glasses.

"We cannot give up without first having exhausted all our resources." Those were Eric's words. He had adopted them from the best motivators in the world. Among them were Napoleon Hill, Max Lucado, Jack Canfield, Stephen Covey, and others.

"Besides," Vivienne continued, "we're going to save money. We will not eat in restaurants again. We will not go to movies any more. We will tell Joaquina to stop coming to clean the house and wash our clothes. We will learn how to cook, clean house, and take care of our clothes. Right, Turner?"

After his jaw dropped, Turner started kicking the floor. The situation at home had gone from bad to ridiculous! He still had trouble tying his tennis shoe laces. Cleaning house and washing clothes seemed so complicated without mentioning, boring!

For the next three days, Eric's smile faded from his face and Alexandra stopped floating across the floor. Now she seemed to be dragging her feet like a chained slave who is pushed by a master to do undesirable chores.

I must stop watching so many documentaries about slavery, Vivienne thought, biting her lower lip. Her lips were swollen from her new habit of pulling the skin of her lips with her teeth until they bled.

Claudia Carbonell

After her parents gave her good night kisses and the house went silent, she brought her computer to bed, put on her earphones and watched documentary after documentary about slaves. It was a bitter obsession. She knew that by remaining connected to the slave kids through those images, she would keep alive her mission of helping them.

Buddy left her feet and laid down next to her, watching her eyes closely. He wanted to make sure they were dry at all times.

Night fell, yawning its icy breath. With its cloak, it covered the moon and all brightness from the firmament. An orchestra of crickets intensified the groans and the weeping of the thirteen boys of Gahate who were now inhabiting a village as unknown as it was bitter. Already one of them named Chintak, a 12-year old boy, had died.

"Aatish," said Ballabh," if you concentrate only on the noise of the crickets, you won't hear the kids' crying as much."

"Just try to sleep," whispered Aatish. "Tomorrow will be another day of hard work."

Ballabh shivered. His back could no longer bear the weight of those huge slabs of stone. His shoulders were as cracked as the soles of his feet. Aatish had ripped the skin of the big toes where the toe strap of his sandal rested. Ballabh's feet soles were so broken that it hurt more to wear his sandals than to walk barefoot.

"Tomorrow, we will wear our grandfather's shoes. Those will protect our feet," Aatish proposed.

"Oh, that's right. We have Grandpa's shoes," Ballabh agreed, widening his eyes. "With them, you will not feel pain on your feet, Aatish. They are very comfortable."

As always, they were lying on their stomachs. The back and shoulder pain didn't allow them to lie on their backs or sideways. They wore their entire wardrobe and their grandfather's to shield them from the burning cold. Just like in their village, they breathed under the tent and had their faces covered with Grandma's scarf.

"How do you think Mommy and Granny are doing?" Ballabh asked in a broken voice. "I miss them."

"Sleep now or the old wicked man will beat you to death just as he did with Chintak."

"That's not true. He did not kill him," Ballabh whispered. "Chintak tried to run away and a tiger ate him."

"Don't be stupid. That's what he wants us to believe but I know the truth. Everyone knows it, but no one wants to admit it out of fear."

Aatish had what happened to Chintak fresh in his memory from that morning; ninety-seven days since they were recruited.

Chintak looked very tired. He complained about his back and kept crying.

He dragged himself down from the steep hill to unload a slab next to Devang's truck. This is where they loaded them at the end of the workday.

Once again, he was back down, bringing the last slab. He lifted the strap from his head and dropped it to the ground while the other kids were beginning to load the truck. Chintak slid his fingers under the slab and began to tremble. With all his strength, he tried to lift the block of stone but instead moans blurted out of his mouth.

He placed a hand at the bottom of his back and pushed it in as if he was arranging the vertebrae in place. He sunk to the ground, held his knees, and laid with his face towards the moon. He rocked from side to side, massaging his vertebrae against the harsh ground.

As Devang was stepping out of the dark slaves' sleeping facility, he shouted, "Stand up!"

"I cannot, sir," groaned Chintak.

"I've repeated it several times before. Call me master!" He unfastened his terrible black buffalo strap, and with it struck him twice in the arms. The strongest flap fell on his back.

Chintak tried to rise. The pain disfigured his face. Several boys approached him, eager to help; among them were the Singh brothers.

"Go back to work, all of you! Let this sluggard stand up by himself," shouted Devang. "Let's see how much of a big boy you are. On your feet."

Chintak straightened his back, sat up, but at the moment he was about to flex his knees, they started wobbling and the extreme exhaustion pushed him sideways. Devang lifted him up like an old rag and threw him into the cargo box of the truck, which was full of slabs, and drove away. The boys trembled. Surely, the blow had broken a bone. The next day, Devang returned, saying that the ungrateful boy had tried to escape and when he was coming down the mountain, a tiger attacked him.

Aatish could not sleep throughout the night, although with all his strength he yearned to close his eyes and forget about everything! Erase from his mind that day when he left his village with his brother. The journey took ten hours and Devang only stopped the vehicle once to urinate in the surrounding shrubbery of a farmhouse. The boys jumped to do the same. The intense cold and absolute hunger made their bellies growl.

The brothers, who were sitting under the back glass of the truck, on several occassions knocked on it to call on Devang's attention.

He stared at them through the rearview mirror and, judging from the bulge of his dark eye circles, the kids could clearly see that he was laughing.

From a picnic hamper on the passenger seat, he took out sandwiches and canned drinks. During the whole trip, he was eating and drinking.

Aatish's guts knotted at the thought of his Grandma's words. She had believed so much in that horrible sheep-dressed wolf.

"We better jump out of the truck!" he insisted, "This guy is going to kill us!" But no one heard him. The other kids, including Ballabh, claimed that Devang was as his name defined him in the Indian language, a *man of God.*

They climbed a steep mountain. To one side was a cliff, the bottom of which was strewn by a river. The cold intensified and the kids wrapped themselves in blankets. Those whose family had been nomads, as was the case of the Singh brothers, hid under their tents. At dusk, the truck came to a halt.

They were beside a massive rock jail-like construction of a large city, with two insulting tiny windows. An iron bar door that hid the bleak cemented floor where the kids were about to lie on their tummies to weep, and chatter their teeth from their sore backs, injured shoulders, dented skulls, and cracked feet, during their sporadic sleep of every night. Once Aatish realized the torturous future they were about to endure, he shouted, "This man has taken us as slaves!"

As always, Vivienne was still bringing out the lemonade stand, while her friends distributed flyers throughout the neighborhood. On Saturdays, the family cleaned the house. Alexandra washed the five bathrooms and the kitchen. Eric vacuumed the first floor, Vivienne did the second, and Turner dusted and polished the furniture.

Alexandra and Vivienne dusted off the cover of the cookbook that a friend gave Eric and Alexandra as their wedding gift. They both planned a weekly menu for the whole month. The ingredients of their meals were inexpensive, nutritious, and almost always, edible.

One Wednesday after class, when Alexandra had dismissed the students from the house, Eric left his office. His eyes were glowing and he was allowing a shy glimpse of a smile to escape.

"I've contacted thirty former clients and proposed them to be our investors for the lemonade stand. Nine of them accepted! We will have enough money to continue with your mission, princess."

Vivienne screamed and threw herself at Eric and hugged him with all her strength. He almost fell backwards.

The first to accept the offer was a young man who had inherited a lot of money from his recently deceased father. He had already wasted part of the fortune gambling in the casinos of Las Vegas. Now, he wanted to do something that his father would have been proud of with what was left. It had to be a noble cause. Vivienne's mission was exactly that.

Alexandra designed the label of the lemonade bottles. It had a circle and in its center were several hearts. Around them, eleven people with smiling faces of all races holding hands seemed to be dancing. The name of the trademark was written above the drawing which read *Make a Change, Organic Lemonade. The funds will help put an end to child slavery.* Vivienne had insisted on including a chain-shaped medal to each bottle with another brief message: *Each lemonade frees slaves.*

They bought twenty thousand more bottles and ingredients. In the Harr's kitchen, the whole family and the new investor took turns squeezing lemons, measuring agave nectar, and mixing everything up. They spent their entire days working.

Meanwhile, Eric called each Pleasanton store to tell them the story of the delicious lemonade with a great cause. Whole Foods and Mollie Stone's were their first customers.

Vivienne wanted to distribute the first order of her bottled lemonade to Whole Foods. It was one of her favorite supermarkets, owing to their organic produce and their guarantee that their food was free of synthetic and genetically modified ingredients.

Next to other natural drinks, *Make a Change Organic Lemonade* stood out like a classy lady dressed in colorful attire and decorated with a chain around her neck.

Now, instead of bringing out her lemonade stand, Vivienne, Turner, and Alexandra, visited Whole Foods to serve samples of lemonade in tiny cups to potential customers. After a couple of months, sales tripled. Eric stayed home negotiating with other stores and persuading the bank to wait. They would soon start paying the mortgage. He had faith that soon new clients would be knocking on his door.

The new daily routine of the Harr family was more or less as follows:

- Get up at 6:30 a.m.

- Shower and get dressed.

- Go to the kitchen to make breakfast.

Claudia Carbonell

Turner read the day's menu and took out from the refrigerator the ingredients to be used to prepare the three meals of the day. He tossed the frozen meats in a bowl of water to thaw them. He washed breakfast fruit, the potatoes and other vegetables for dinner.

• Vivienne mixed the breakfast ingredients. Beat the eggs, or prepare the dough for the pancakes, and squeeze the oranges for the juice.

• Alexandra placed the pans on the stove and cooked the food that Vivienne had previously mixed. Vivienne was also vigilant that nothing got burnt.

• Once finished, Eric washed the dishes and Alexandra cleaned the kitchen.

• Eric spent the rest of the day in his office promoting lemonade sales and tweeting about the progress of the business, while the kids attended their classes taught by Alexandra. In addition, twice a week they went to their YMCA for gym and swimming lessons.

All the rest of the house chores were divided into four equal parts. The food continued improving and the culinary channel of the world's most famous chefs became Alexandra's favorite shows. From those shows, she copied recipes for the family menu.

The charm of staying very busy performing a labor of love is that time goes by like the cool breeze of Northern California.

Twitter, the famous social networking platform was about to become public. Richard William Costolo, the president of Twitter, invited Vivienne to ring the bell of the New York Stock Exchange.

In the middle of hundreds of screens with the blue bird logo and millions of numbers, Vivienne rang the bell and Twitter's president toasted with a bottle of lemonade from *Make a Change.*

The next day, the Harrs returned home. Naturally, the family was tired, and what better way to rest than taking a walk in the woods? Vivienne proposed a walk to Turner and in seconds he was ready with his torn jeans from last year, and his dad's fine cashmere sweater that Alexandra had shrunk when she tossed it in the dryer. Mom and Dad settled on the sofa of the living room with the TV remote control in front of them. Buddy was ready with his leash between his teeth, wagging his tail at the front door.

"Don't worry, Buddy, we won't leave without you," Vivienne promised, stuffing in her backpack three plastic bags which contained an open can of dog food and two chicken sandwiches for her and Turner.

Claudia Carbonell

"Don't run, children," Alexandra warned. "It has rained and there's mud." "All right, Mommy," Vivienne agreed, and they hurried into the woods.

The emerald-green grass was mixed with slippery neon moss which smelled like green tea. Further in, the ground was covered with leaves that had fallen from deciduous and evergreen trees. It was easy to identify the leaves belonging to each type of tree by its size and shape.

Lizards jumped over the roots of the trees and climbed their trunks, frightened by the visitors.

The current of a running brook added music to the orchestra of thousands of birds. The luscious smell of wet soil and the mentholated fragrance of eucalyptus obligated them to breathe deeply and to stretch their arms to the sides to simulate flight.

Miranda the deer peered at the kids from several feet away. She was hidden behind a massive sequoia. Buddy saw her and started jumping like a rabbit on steroids. Vivienne maneuvered Buddy's leash but his strength was greater than hers and he took off towards Miranda. As the kids followed their pet, the deer's short tail was barely visible in the distance. The dog's barks mingled with howls.

"That howl is not Buddy's!" Turner warned.

Vivienne felt the collapse of her heart to the belly. Her brother's auditory sense was unequivocal.

Claudia Carbonell

"Buddy, come back!" Vivienne called. Her eyes began to water. "Dumb dog! "What is it that howls?" She asked, gripping Turner's hand tightly.

"I don't know," Turner lied, not to frighten Vivienne any further, though he knew they were coyotes.

The kids kept running in the direction of the howls that were now combined with the dog's shrieks.

"Oh no, Buddy! Buddy! cried out Vivienne, accelerating their sprint. Turner was holding his tears to keep his sister from increasing her worry. Beads of sweat sprouted from their foreheads and their hands were slippery.

Now Buddy was racing back toward them followed by three medium-sized dogs. Vivienne recognized they were coyotes. When these wild dogs are hungry, they eat all kinds of animals, including kids. Vivienne's hands took on the agility of humming bird wings as she took the briefcase, unzipped the zipper, and seized the three bags of food.

The coyotes were in front of them. Two had gray fur and one mahogany. Their tails dropped, their hair stood on end, and their brown eyes fixed on the children. Buddy positioned himself in front of his masters and ducked his head, ready to launch at these enemies.

"AAAAA!" Vivienne uttered a deafening scream and threw the plastic bags of treats to the three beasts. She grabbed Buddy's leash, pulled Turner by the hand, and rushed into the brook.

"Don't let go, Turner!" she warned and turned her stare to the coyotes. They had already removed all the contents of each bag and were devouring and fighting for the food. Once the trio crossed the brook, the coyotes stared straight at it. Their actions were synchronized as if they were one body. Vivienne knew they were preparing to cross the stream to continue with the main dish. Now the beasts' eyes were fixed on Turner.

"You'll have to eat me first, devils! Run faster," she demanded.

A few feet away was the gate of their neighbor's property. The coyotes had slowed down. The water seemed to have placated their eagerness. The kids arrived at the Gutierrez family's barbed-wire fence. Nelson Gutierrez overheard Vivienne's screams and hurried to the fence as she lifted Turner over it. He shouted, "I can go up alone. Vivienne, climb over the fence!"

Nelson's eyes almost popped out of their sockets as he got a load of the coyotes. They were about twenty feet away from them.

"Holy God!" he shouted in a broken English. He bent down and grabbed a fallen eucalyptus branch.

With it, he stuck out an arm from the fence and, swinging it madly, shouted, "Get out of here! Shoo, shoo, out of here!"

The coyotes shot off. Nelson helped lift Vivienne over the fence, and she lifted Buddy. He helped by bending his knees. Even in a state of panic, he kept his sanity.

"Thank you very much, sir!" said Vivienne, sinking her teeth into her lips, digging for some loose skin to pull.

"Children, why are you alone in the woods?" Nelson asked while studying them closely, "You are Eric Harr's children, aren't you?"

Turner felt uneasy to have been recognized since it was only a matter of seconds for their parents to find out what had happened. Now, they wouldn't have permission to return alone to the forest.

"Please don't tell our parents!" Turner pleaded. His face turned the color of a radish; between red and fuchsia with a splash of blue over his upper lip. He was sweating and his rising fear made his teeth chatter. Today was the most fun he had in a long, long time. Yet it could be taken away from him permanently if the neighbor informed their parents.

Vivienne faced Turner. The neighbor was right. It was dangerous to be alone in the forest.

Nevertheless, if their parents found out what had happened, they could never return to the woods. *Pity, it's my favorite place after Knotts Berry Farm, and it's always an adventure to explore it with Turner,* Vivienne thought. She wanted mightily to beg Nelson to keep silent, but it would not be a good example for her brother who always saw her as his role model.

"Turner, Mr. Gutierrez is right. It is dangerous to walk alone in the woods."

"It is my duty to let your parents know of this incident. I'm sorry," Nelson replied.

"I understand," answered Vivienne, blushing. "Do what your heart tells you to do." It was a phrase similar to the one that brought her the biggest sales of lemonade. Possibly, he would not say anything. After all, he seemed to be a compassionate man.

"Okay, I'll take you back home," he said taking them by the hand and tucking Buddy's leash-bracelet on his wrist.

"Thank you, but that's not necessary," Vivienne insisted.

"Ah, he's going to get us in trouble!" Turner complained.

"I don't think so," said Nelson, "I know your father. Not personally, but in interviews. I've followed him since he won his first race on November 11, 1993.

111

He's a humble man with a big heart. And what he loves most in life is his family." He stared at them. Judging by his playful behavior, Buddy felt comfortable with this neighbor.

With each step, Buddy crossed in front of them. On two occasions he stood on his hind legs and put his front ones on Nelson's chest. His garden was as large as theirs. In his acre of land, he grew plantains from Colombia, his native country and tomate de árbol. "It is a very sour fruit," he explained, "it's used for making juice." He also had a few Asian fruit trees, such as white zapote, lichee, and mangosteen. Although he only got a few of those exotic Asian fruits each year, it was worth to take care of them in exchange for the most exquisite natural dessert in the planet.

He pointed out those trees with pride. They looked as appetizing as bare chicken bones.

"Don't let the appearance fool you," he explained. "Let me prove it to you." He rushed to one of the bare branches where several birds were jumping on a twig and fluttering around.

"I'm sorry, guys," he apologized, stretching his arm right in the middle of the bird reunion and grabbing a yellow, pear-shaped fruit. A number of the winged gatherers, a Western blue bird and a Northern flicker among them, pecked his hand.

"It's their favorite fruit, as it is mine. This is a white zapote and it comes from Vietnam."

He reached near the end of the fence where a broken sprinkler was squirting water and washed the fruit. He then returned with a wide smile and proposed, "Taste it and tell me what you think," while handing it to Vivienne.

She passed it to Turner. He didn't know what to do with it. It had several tiny holes where the birds had stuck their beaks. He inserted the nail of his pinky finger to clean around each one of those holes and bit a piece. Buddy was slobbering, watching the fruit and going up on his hind legs to give it a better look.

"It tastes like candy!" cheered Turner and brought the fruit close to Vivienne's mouth. The zapote was melting between his fingers.

Vivienne took a small bite. It had the flesh of a ripe avocado as if smothered in agave nectar.

"Umm, delicious," she claimed.

"I told you," affirmed Nelson.

When the fruit was gone and the flat seeds were stripped from all flesh, Turner allowed Buddy to lick his hand.

Once they reached the front door of the Harrs' house and Nelson rang the bell, Turner released Nelson's hand and ran to shelter behind a Catalpa. Buddy barked and Eric opened the door. He was crying. "Children!" he sputtered.

"I'm sorry, Dad!" Vivienne shouted and hugged him. "We won't go alone to the woods again."

"Oh, my little one, where is Turner?" He asked, then noticed Nelson.

"I'm Eric," he said, wiping his tears with the sleeve of his left arm and extending his right hand towards Nelson's. The neighbor hesitated to shake the hand of one of his favorite athletes of all time.

"Come, Turner," Vivienne called. *Dad seems happy, but why the tears?* She thought. She's seen him weeping a few times. When he cried the most was the day Turner was born. Other times she saw tears in his eyes was three years ago when her Mom won the National Art Award. A few months back he cried when Turner won first place at the Tae Kwon Do Academy, and the moment he set eyes on the lemonade bottles before going to market.

"How's Mom?" She asked.

"She's great, so great."

Turner settled in next to Buddy. Although it was rare when his parents scolded him, Buddy as always, was ready to impose order.

Nelson finally shook Eric's hand. He did so by grabbing it with both of his hands.

"The great pleasure is mine," he said, smiling broadly. "Congratulations, you have two lovely children, and a very intelligent dog." His Hispanic accent was very heavy yet it had the joyous ring of a bell.

"You're so kind, thank you," Eric replied. No matter how hard he tried to hold back the tears, they were bursting non stop, like Nelson's broken sprinkler. "My apologies, Nelson, I just received this news that left me, well; perplexed, and immensely happy."

"Daddy," insisted Vivienne. "What happened?"

"Princess," whispered Eric. "The, the, oh, no" tears kept streaming down his face.

Buddy began to feel the tension so he threw himself upside down at Eric's feet. It was urgent to call on the master's attention to help him calm down.

Vivienne and Turner hugged him. "Excuse me, Nelson and children, but these are tears of joy. I just got some wonderful news. Please, Nelson, come in, come in," he insisted. He directed him into the living room, dragging his feet so he wouldn't step on his pet who didn't for one instant stop rolling on his back over his shoes.

"Alex," he called, "please come and visit with our neighbor while I take something from the office."

Alexandra hurried to the living room and introduced herself. Eric headed to his office.

Vivienne stared at her mother's face. She looked radiant and her smile couldn't be wider.

"We are coming with you, Daddy," Vivienne said and rushed behind Eric with Turner on her heels. Their hearts were still throbbing after the confrontation with the coyotes.

He placed both hands on his fine rosewood desk, grabbed a letter in his trembling hands and started reading, pausing after every sentence: *"Dear Harr family ..."* From there, the warm contents became nectar to their ears. At the end, Vivienne's heart almost exploded, and rightly so for that letter was a personal invitation from Pope Francis. He was inviting her and her family to attend a Peace Summit in the Vatican. She had to deliver a speech.

Wow! Her journey was taking the form of a science fiction story, beginning with the impossible dream of the protagonist to end child slavery. What's a story without villains? This story had four insufferable bad guys in the form of school bullies who made Vivienne's life miserable. The test: to raise the sum of $150,000 to initially free 500 slaves proved the protagonist's determination to her mission.

Almost having lost her house made Vivienne realize the commitment of a united family fighting for the same ideal. The recognition from the media and the public showed that many believed in her.

Today, she was being invited to the private residence of one of her heroes, Pope Francis, to speak in front of the entire world. This was not even possible in a fairy tale! All these thoughts but in great mess made her head throb.

What? She, I mean me; Vivienne Harr, invited by the Pope to speak in front of him! This thought was threatening to cause her head to explode.

"Princess," explained Eric, "you will speak in front of government leaders, Nobel Prize recipients, scientists, members of the United Nations, and celebrities. You will be part of 50 people who are fighting for a better world and will be delivering their message to the ears of the Pope."

Buddy went berserk barking.

The color of Vivienne's face changed from pink to blue and her lips turned as white as the zapote she had just tasted.

She was too stunned to respond to Turner's insistent questions: "Who is the Pope? What is the Vatican? And why does Vivienne look so weird?"

Vivienne placed her trembling hand on her chest and whispered, "I can't speak before such an important audience!" She meant that she lacked the ability to express herself eloquently, that she lacked the intelligence of the other 49 prominent members of the conference. This conference that would be seen by the entire world! Besides, *she was just a little girl, a little girl.* Her mother's words and the mocking voices of the school bullies echoed in her ears. The office began to turn and the floor to swell. With both hands she clung to the edge of the desk.

"I can't speak in front of the Pope!" once again she insisted.

"Who is the Pope?" Turner demanded, kicking the floor.

While Eric was explaining to Turner who the Supreme Pastor of the Catholic Church was, Vivienne's heart – instead of throbbing – was kicking, eager to escape into the deepest part of the forest and give up its function. It was a challenge to keep pumping blood throughout the body while the nervous system was wallowing like a little child with a temper tantrum.

"This is a great honor, my dear," said Eric. "Imagine having the opportunity to speak before the High Pontiff who will send your message to the entire world."

"Eric, Eric," Alexandra called. He hurried out.

"How embarrassing. The neighbor left and you didn't talk to him. Why did it you take so long?" Vivienne could barely hear her mother's words. She sat on Eric's swivel-upholstered mahogany chair. The office was spinning to the right so she started whirling in the opposite direction to neutralize the dizziness which was making her nauseous.

Stacked rocks. That was the perpetual vision of the child slaves who were property of the man who called himself *man of God*. Every day, from dawn until the moon was up, the children took rocks, set them on their backs, hiked down the hill and installed them next to the truck to finally deposit them inside the cargo box of the vehicle.

Today at dawn, a man arrived, driving a truck as gray as the day. It rained and Devang demanded the children stand against the wall of the recruitment building.

"These are my boys," Devang's words pierced Aatish's ears. "Choose three. I shall soon return to the village from which I collected them to replace them with others." How eager the kids were to become a bald eagle and fly back to their village to quack to the villagers not to let them be fooled again.

The man had a lot in common with Devang; huge bulging eyes enhanced with an evil glow in the center and rimmed with deep dark circles. They wore identical white robes.

The clothes didn't have a single stain on them. They had large, pointed bellies which contrasted with the flat ones of the children.

The slaves already had the bags tied on their backs where the slabs of rocks were carried and the bands on their heads to help them support the weight. The man stared at each boy from head to toe. They all had their necks sunk in as if they were already carrying the rocks, shoulders down and eyes focused on the ground.

"Everyone looks weak," assessed the stranger as he strolled from one end of the line to the other. He returned and squeezed each one of the kids' arms to determine if there was any muscle. He also examined their calves and backs. In both places he felt the mass of muscle produced by the hundreds of times they went up and down the mountain while carrying the heavy rocks on their backs.

"I'll take these two," he said, touching Dipak's and Daman's shoulders. They were brothers. He scrutinized them closely, narrowed his eyes and added, "Umm, on second thought, I'll just take this one," and pulled Dipak away from the group. Daman howled disconsolately.

"Silence!" Devang yelled, unfastening his belt.

"How much will you charge me for him, brother?" the man asked.

"In the market, they're worth $200, but because it's for you I'll only charge you $100. Ah, but on one condition. On your next trip to the villages, bring me about four Kamalari from seven to nine years old. This village needs a few little girls to take care of me."

The stranger laughed, pulled a wallet out of the back pocket of his pants, and handed Devang two $50 bills.

Daman lifted the band from his head and wiped away his tears. He frowned and fixed a long stare at his brother who was being pushed by the slave buyer to his car.

The acquisition of the slave had interrupted the kids' meager breakfast which consisted of Del Bhat's: rice and lentils without seasoning. The children prepared it on an outside fire pit of wood and rocks. Devang kept two sacks of these two grains inside the recruit room where the slaves slept.

From a deep well, the kids drew water into a bucket, from which they bathed and drank. The water had a slightly salty taste which made them more thirsty. Aatish imagined it was the sweat of them all buried deep in that mountain of death.

At dusk, Ballabh could no longer bear the slab on his back.

Little by little, step by step, he climbed uphill to reach the top where the endless row of blocks of rocks, awaited and brought one down to the area where the master's truck was parked.

Right there, a few feet from where they slept every night away from Granny and Mom. Next to the stack of wood where they cooked and ate lentils and rice twice a day. He missed his village to the point of feeling like he was going crazy. Each memory brought a sharp pain from the tip of his ragged toes to the top of his head. It was unbearable to think about the games with Aatish, and above all, the pampering from their two moms.

Panting, he stopped beside the top step made of the same stone slab that he daily carried and dropped his gaze. How different was the view from the one of his village with the enormous cascades of water, the carpet of clouds, and the panorama of the houses scattered in the inferior terraces. His home had the best view of all. It crowned the mountain and touched the sky.

"I can't take one more step." Dangerous tears streamed down his cheeks and the freezing breeze pushed them down into the cliff. He moved away from the stairs to allow the other children to descend with their loads of stones.

"Get back to work or the master will beat you to death," Daman whispered. His gaze had turned vague, as if the light of his eyes had been turned off.

Two cross-like-shaped wrinkles had formed on his forehead above the bridge of the nose.

At that moment, a purple flash with blue and magenta hues surged from behind a pile of rock. It was a redhead monal. It lifted its emerald crest and stared sharply at Aatish.

It rushed to the precipice and halfway down the mountain, it took flight. There were many monals in his village. The villagers suspected that the residue of one of them had caused the death of his father.

The monal landed on a car which was parked next to the master's vehicle. It seemed that a woman with long, shiny blond hair was coming out of the vehicle followed by three men. She spoke briefly with Devang, offered him her hand, hurried to the foot of the mountain, and began to climb. Aatish approached Ballabh.

"Are your feet also burning?" he asked. They always burned, but today the brothers felt double the pain, the sting, and the burn.

"Yes," he answered. They were both wearing their grandfather's big shoes. They weighed almost as much as a brick and it cost them double the struggle to raise their feet. When lowering them, the shoes plummeted abruptly as if having minds of their own.

Again and again, they almost lost their balance and yet miraculously they didn't roll over the precipice.

"Perhaps it won't be a bad idea to fall off the cliff and end the pain of our bodies, especially of our hearts, thought Aatish while staring at the monal.

The visiting lady was now stepping on the top of the mountain. Aatish placed an arm around Ballabh's shoulder. In better times he would've squeezed it tightly but today Aatish barely skimmed his brother's shoulder with his arm. Their shoulders stung as much as their feet.

Life hurt badly. It was as heavy as the rocks. Aatish was willing to jump off the cliff if the woman were a slave buyer and wanted to take one of them away. They could never be separated. Now they only had each other.

The woman stood behind them.

Click, click, were the sounds they heard behind their backs.

They both turned to face her. She was taking pictures of them. As she lowered the lens of the big camera, they were perplexed by her angelic beauty, her bright blue eyes and her hopeful smile.

She said, "I'm Lisa Kristine. I thank you boys for this photograph. I promise you that these photos will go around the world. Through them you will tell the world your story."

Today, Vivienne had taken out her lemonade stand to the road that crossed her street with the main road, Milliken Drive. In a couple of hours, there would be a parade of antique cars on Milliken Drive which would attract a large crowd. Beside the stand, Vivienne had placed a chalkboard where she announced the sale of lemonade in bright pink letters.

In the meantime, she was preparing the speech to deliver at the Peace Conference in front of the Pope. By her feet was a waste basket overflowing with rolled papers tucked in underneath the stand. She had stapled an old curtain all around the back of the stand to cover the waste basket, her school books, and some of her brother's toys.

Turner, with his head nested inside his arms, couldn't look more bored.

Buddy kept vigilant on Vivienne's eyes to dry them with his tongue whenever tears welled up. These rolled down her face every now and then, whenever she couldn't find the perfect words for her speech while reminding herself how dumb she was.

Uuf, uff! Buddy barked. Three people were running down the street. Buddy leaped to investigate the commotion. It was a woman and two boys.

"Buddy, come back!" Vivienne shouted, looking both ways before crossing the street. Her dog was already next to those people and was barking at them.

Turner, in a leap, was standing by Vivienne's side. If she crossed the street, she would do it with him. "They're the school bullies, Franco and Rebecca," Turner assured.

"True, it's them," Vivienne concluded, grabbing her brother's hand and running after them calling Buddy. The lady stopped, panting and holding onto a light pole.

Sorry, ma'am," said Vivienne. "Do you need help?"

Franco was crying while Rebecca was frowning at the street. The three of them were sweating and seemed exhausted.

"Immigration patrols are following us. They have already captured my husband!" the woman whispered, taking her head in both hands.

"Follow me to the stand!" proposed Vivienne, grabbing Buddy's leash and Turner's hand.

Once in front of the stand she demanded, "Hurry, go underneath," as she raised the curtain. "Turner, appeared calm at all times. Buddy, be quiet; lie down next to me and don't stare under the stand, you hear me?"

Shrieking, Buddy obeyed Vivienne's orders. However, every time he heard the strangers whimpering beneath the table, he pushed his nose underneath the curtain, to sniff. Meanwhile, Turner fixed a static grin showing his teeth.

A black Volvo S90 turned the corner of the street and slowly approached them.

"It's them. Turner, be casual," ordered Vivienne.

"I am," he replied, widening his grin.

Even though the windows were quite dark, she could see the silhouettes of three men: the driver, the passenger in the front seat, and one behind. *The man in the back must be Rebecca and Franco's dad,* Vivienne thought.

"Good morning children," saluted the gentleman sitting at the driver's side window, lowering the glass halfway. He was wearing black sunglasses. The driver was wearing identical ones. "Are you preparing for the parade?" he asked, glancing at the lemonade jug.

"Yes sir," replied Vivienne. "We do it for a cause, to free the child slaves of the world."

"How nice," he whispered, lowering his glasses halfway on the bridge of his nose and holding his gaze on her for a few seconds. "We're looking for a woman and two kids; a girl and a boy. Have you seen them running down this street?" He asked, peering down Harmony Lane.

"No, sir," replied Vivienne, glancing at the back seat passenger through the open window. He was a middle-aged man, crying and kissing a necklace with a crucifix around his neck.

"Thank you," said the man, and the car moved a few inches forward while the passenger in front stared down Harmony Street. Meanwhile, Vivienne was now in front of the passenger sitting in the back, so she grabbed the chalk and wrote on the board:

Elos estan bin.

She did it in Spanish and knew she had misspelled, *They are OK,* but judging by the gentleman's smile, she knew he had understood.

She showed him her two thumbs up. Turner did the same, then the car made a U-turn and drove away.

"They're gone," Vivienne yelled, pulling up the curtain on the table.

"Ay, I'm fainting," moaned the woman, crawling out of the stand followed by the kids.

"Your husband knows you are well. I wrote it on the board and he saw it."

"Thank you, little girl," mumbled the woman while crying.

"Your kids go to school with us," Vivienne said.

Turner's eyes narrowed and he stared at them with aggravation.

"Do you want to stay in my house for a while?" she asked.

Buddy seemed to have understood Vivienne's proposal and set about examining how reliable the strangers might be.

He sniffed their feet and seemed to be biting his tongue to avoid nipping them.

"No child, you are very kind but I don't want to inconvenience you."

Buddy swiped his tail along the legs of the kids' mom in approval.

Franco's and Rebecca's faces were as hot pink as the letters on the board. Not once did they look up to face Vivienne and Turner.

"It's no problem. I'll explain what happened to my parents and Dad will take you home. But first, do you want a glass of lemonade?"

"Yes, thank you," the lady answered. The kids nodded, sipping lemonade before Vivienne took them to her home.

Pieces of mountains, rocks, and piles of sharp pine branches blocked the road to Gahate. The village was reduced to clusters of bricks, rocks, and shattered tiles. The few chickens that had not been killed for their meat, rummaged beneath the collapsed homes for something edible. The arched electrical pole with its dropped wires threatened to decapitate any passerby who dared to cross it.

Devastation. Death. Disappearance of good people. The Raju Lama Foundation had been present bringing food, tents, clothing, and some money to the victims of the earthquake of April 15, 2015.

At ten o'clock, in the secret village where Devang kept his slaves, they still hadn't recovered from the terror of the earthquake which had shaken the village intensely but with less intensity than in Gahate.

"Aatish, if you close your eyes very hard and think of our village, you will remember it as if you had it in front of you," proposed Ballabh who struggled against his exhaustion and his body aches to keep awake.

"You and your silly craving for daydreaming. Now, just go to sleep. Remember, tomorrow is another day of hard work."

"I like being awake to think about our moms. Remember when we played in the brook?" Ballabh squeezed his eyes shut so hard that the memories splashed with stars from his great effort to return to his village. "Granny always brought us broth. It was so tasty. Um, I loved the smell of cilantro and onion."

"Hahaha!" Aatish laughed, "Granny added to the pot of broth stones from the river. She said the rocks..."

"...were full of accumulated minerals from thousands of years which helped keep us strong while added flavor to meals..." They finished the sentence in unison. They had heard it so many times.

"Do you remember the moving bridge above the Indrawati River?" Ballabh asked.

"How could I ever forget it? You always jumped on top of it and once you broke a board. I was horrified. I thought we would end up in the river... with Dad"

"I know, but those monkeys started screaming on the branch of that pine tree which made me feel so happy."

"Ballabh, *everything* brought us joy, remember? Three years have pass..."

They hugged. Daman was listening. He missed his brother who was bought by the slave trader. He also missed his parents, the village with all its fragrance of eucalyptus, surrounded by pine trees, waterfalls, sunflower fields, impregnated with peacefulness, and beauty.

"Keep remembering," he demanded. But the memories had been consumed by tears.

Today Vivienne was at the beauty salon. She had written the speech she would read before the Pope. Writing it had been the most frustrating experience of her entire life. It was also the longest, having taken six terrible months amidst school, work, and interviews. As she waited for her turn, she read and reread her speech. She wanted to memorize it. The next day, she would travel with her family to the Vatican to attend the Peace Summit.

How in the world am I going to be able to talk in front of so many illustrious people? She wondered until she saw stars.

"Vivienne Harr, you can come in now," called one of the girls behind a luxurious glass display counter.

On exhibit were bracelets, watches, necklaces, and pearl earrings that had Vivienne cross-eyed from so much staring.

She stood up and followed the young woman. Vivienne would've liked it if Turner had come with her but presently Eric was taking him to the restroom.

"Do you want me to go with you, darling?" Alexandra asked, putting down on the coffee table a *People* magazine.

"It's not necessary, Mom." She wanted once and for all to prove to her parents that it was unnecessary to be so overprotected by them. Ten months ago, she had turned twelve years of age. In just sixty days, on December 23; she would become a teenager. She clearly wasn't a little girl anymore.

Once Vivienne was seated, she insisted, "Please trim the tips to get rid of my split ends. Oh, and kindly cut my bangs a little bit."

"Of course, miss," replied the girl. "First, I'm going to wash your hair then I'll apply a conditioner to repair all damage." The miraculous balm had the scent of a bouquet of flowers. The girl smothered her scalp with the formula and her silky fingers massaged it and extended the lather to the tips. Vivienne took off her glasses and suddenly, she did not know what happened next.

"You're ready, Miss (she said it in French: mademoiselle.)"

"Oh, thank you," Vivienne answered, grabbing her glasses and examining her hair in the mirror. The girl had tied her hair back. She said goodbye to the other stylists and reached the waiting room where her family was waiting.

"Ah!" a bellow escaped from Alexandra's exaggerated open mouth when she saw her. "Did you want it that short?"

"What do you mean short?" Vivienne protested and ran a hand through her hair. It ended at the nape of the neck instead of the shoulders!

"Nooo!" She shouted horrified. "It cannot be; my hair! Now, what am I going to do?" Crying, she ran out. Turner followed her.

"Little one, wait!" Eric called out chasing after her. "You look beautiful with short hair. I swear."

She, of course, did not believe him. She had never had her hair that short. In three years, her hair had gotten long and improved so much. It was the only thing she thought made her decent-looking. It was now cropped off. She felt as if she had lost a finger or, worse yet, a hand.

Vivienne often hid her face behind her hair. Now, how could she hide? Through the glass of the salon of horrors, she saw her mother arguing with the stylist.

The girl at the counter took out a pearl necklace, arranged it in a box, and handed it to Alexandra. She hurried outside to join her family.

"Look, princess, the salon rewards you for not being satisfied with your haircut with this beautiful pearl necklace," she said, handing the box to her.

"I want to see it," Turner demanded. Vivienne handed him the box and halted in front of her mom.

"Please, let's buy a wig."

"No. You look beautiful," her parents and Turner complimented her while she cried and begged to buy a long hair extension for her trip.

When they returned home, Rebecca, Franco, Amanda, and their mother, told her how great and how much older she looked.

Since the deportation of their father now, they lived at the Harr residence. Every day, they communicated with their patriarch and were planning his return but no one knew how long it would take. He would never cross the Mexican border. He had an attorney whom he was paying a lot of money since he felt it was unfair not to have his family with him. He and his wife came legally into the country and their children were born in the United States.

However, the new president did not seem to mind separating families and was now even proposing to build a wall to prevent the entry of undocumented immigrants into the country.

The night could not have been longer. Vivienne did nothing more than to stare in the mirror, disown her haircut, and be terrified about delivering her speech. The next morning, her dark, dark, circles around her eyes were witness of her insomnia.

"I hope you do well," said Rebecca.

"Good luck," Franco wished her.

They hugged.

"I'm so afraid," Vivienne admitted. "I hope I don't make a fool of myself."

"You won't. You'll be fine," Rebecca assured.

"Have a happy trip and may God be with you," wished Amanda. "Thank you for your hospitality. I cannot believe we will stay in this mansion. You are all angels."

"Mi casa es tu casa. (Our home is yours) Do not forget it," Eric said. He was very grateful that her kids were such good friends to Vivienne. She never revealed anything about past mistakes and had asked Turner and her friends not to say anything against them.

"I'll miss them," Vivienne said.

"I'm only going to miss Buddy," Turner whispered in Vivienne's ear.

The flight took thirteen hours. Vivienne slept sporadically and her heart plummeted each time the plane shuddered. Of all trips, this one had the worst turbulence. The landing was just as terrorizing. Her heart was racing.

Moments later, she was stepping on Italian soil. In 31 minutes, she would enter Vatican City and meet Pope Francis, one of her heroes. He would listen to her speech and the message of the other 49 people of great importance who had been invited.

Her shoulders were heavy. Rushing to stay on par with her parents as they passed Terminal B from Da Vinci Airport to reach the luggage area, the floor began to bulge. She stopped. She had to breathe. So many times, she forgot to do so.

Her parents were talking to her, but she couldn't understand their words. Eric carried her, while Alexandra took Turner in her arms, and they continued walking fast.

Once in the city of Rome, suddenly the knot in Vivienne's belly subsided. She was ecstatic of the city's grandeur, starting with the streets made of dark gray stones, like the cloudy sky.

There were so many fountains, statues, and imposing streets, such as Via della Conciliazione, crowned with the Basilica dome which led them to St. Peter's Basilica and finally to the Vatican City.

Arriving at the Vatican, Turner got very thirsty. Vivienne was so engrossed in her thoughts that she had not felt her dry mouth until Turner complained about his. The taxi suggested stopping in front of the narrow entry way of St. Peter's Square, Piazza Pio XII.

In the middle of a huge gray stone framed with gigantic columns, the taxi driver pointed to the fabulous fountain and said, "Go, you can drink from it." He was from New York City and of course, spoke English, so it was not possible to mistake his assertion.

"But the water from a fountain cannot be safe to drink," Vivienne objected. She well knew that the water must first be filtered. The lemonade water she prepared came out from five gallon jars equipped with a faucet dispenser.

"We are in Rome where we can safely drink from almost any fountain."

Before Vivienne accepted his suggestion, she asked him how long he had been living in Rome and asked him to explain the water-filtering process in the city.

"The water is perfectly filtered and flows straight from the aqueduct," the driver reassured.

Turner was impatient and wanted to open the car door and run to the fountain.

"All right, come on," Vivienne was convinced.

"Will you wait for us, please?" Eric asked and opened the door. He took Alexandra's hand, followed by the kids who rushed to the well. In handfuls, they drank from the fountain. Vivienne had never drunk water with her hands before. She always used a glass. The water was freezing and so refreshing.

Vivienne remembered the pool at her YMCA where she swam. During the summer, it was a delight being refreshed while swimming the backstroke, gazing at the sky, stretching her whole body, and feeling full, which was for her the very definition of freedom.

Next to the Basilica stood Domus Sanctae Marthae, Pope Francis' private residence. Pope Francis had refused to live in the Apostolic Palace and preferred the guest house to have better contact with priests and bishops who worked in the Vatican. As well as, it brought him closer to guests at conferences and meetings, such as the Peace Summit where Vivienne was about to participate. The magnificent alabaster and ivory building, accented by hundreds of windows, contrasted with the colorful attire of the two guards standing on either side of the wide door.

Turner laughed at the guards' attire. He could not imagine that such an ensemble was not a Halloween costume. Vivienne blushed, thinking that the guards might have heard Turner's indiscretion, and explained to him that the guards' blue and yellow striped uniforms with a red cap had originated in the year 1506 and had hardly changed.

Eric squeezed Turner's hand and asked him to remain quiet. Turner didn't understand why they were so worried about his questions. He just wanted to know why in the world they dressed so funny and yet managed such serious expressions.

Once the guards opened the door, the kids gasped. It seemed like the entrance to heaven. The snow-white marble floors with gray stripes in hexagonal form begged to be slid on. Two other guards took their bags and led them to their rooms. One with two wide beds was for Turner and his parents while Vivienne had her own suite!

As her parents and brother were settling in, she jumped onto her bed and laid there. At that moment, she stopped thinking about her speech and contemplated the simple surroundings. The walls were painted white. There was a narrow bed, and next to it, a bedside table made of cedar wood with a Bible on top of it.

The only ornament was a wooden crucifix hanging on the wall above the bed, which reminded her where she was and the mission she had to help those who carried the heaviest crosses on their backs.

Turner did not have time to protest about not having his own room. He had something more urgent to do. His feet itched, or rather, his shoes wanted to dart away! He removed his shoes. He had on his cotton white socks. He knocked on Vivienne's room and invited her outside.

On each side of the hallway was a line of guards. Their eyes were fixed on the wall directly in front of them and seemed hypnotized. Turner crouched and stepped away from Vivienne's door as quiet as the hopping of a rabbit. Once he was several feet away from the guard next to his sister's room, he reared himself back and threw all his weight forward and slid down the hall. He kept sliding, imagining he was on an ice rink. Once he reached the end of the corridor, he slid back. He noticed that the guards were not reacting to his deeds. They kept their eyes transfixed and expressionless on the front wall.

Vivienne went on the lookout at either side of the hallway. She approached the guard next to her suite and waved her hand in front of his face. It was obvious that he only noticed the wall in front of him which motivated her to take off her shoes.

She also had socks on that begged to be given a better use and her brain craved a needed break. With a big smile, she joined Turner on the rink. Holding hands, they threw themselves in the direction of their rooms.

All of a sudden, without warning, right in front of her suite, a door flung ajar. No one other than Pope Francis himself, escorted by four guards, headed out. Vivienne and Turner landed at his feet. Vivienne lifted her popped-out eyes and saw the right hand of her hero, reaching out to her. She remembered the greeting protocol to the Holy Pontiff. She put her chapped lips on it and kissed his ring.

The Pope laughed and bellowed, "That greeting is unacceptable. This is how it's done," he crouched down and held Vivienne and Turner in a tight embrace.

In a secret village of Nepal, each slave was depositing the pile of stones they had brought down from the mountain that day. Ballabh's left shoulder was bleeding, however, he did not complain. He knew that if he did, there was a chance that Devang would sell him to bring another better slave in his place. No one dared to ask for the name of the village they were at, especially when they were coming back home.

His master had already got rid of four of them, including Daman who climbed into the truck of his new master, crying tears of joy in hopes that he would perhaps be reunited with his brother.

Devang had bought seven slaves from a lord who boasted of having obtained his slaves from villages where people had grown up in slavery for several generations.

"Therefore," explained the lord, these "programmed" kids are better than camels because they have the power to understand orders. They never complain, not once do they get hurt, nor do they get tired. Best of all, they never had contact with family members or knew a toy, so their only recreation is work and obeying their master."

Aatish's blood jumped to his cheeks when he heard this while Ballabh struggled to follow the "programmed" slaves' way of working. It was impossible. They were twice as fast, skilled, and strong. Their faces had no expression. They did not mutter a word, nor did they set eyes on anyone. They resembled robots instead of human beings. The only semblance they had of children was their stature, yet their movements, the absence of gestures, their large humps, and the downward lips belonged to a humanoid race.

Aatish also unconsciously wanted to be on par with the new slaves. It was unpredictable how his master would get rid of them. Would he sell them? Kill them? Worst yet, would he separate him from his brother?

Devang watched them at all times and shouted, "Useless slaves! Get moving sluggards! Learn from the new group. They are productive." The few times they could breathe deeply were when the master's talkative device rang and he spoke to it. During these moments, they took longer breaths and gave themselves a few extra seconds to lift the next slab. At nighttime, the soles of their feet burned as if they were walking on fire.

Aatish had two broken corns on the sole of his right foot through which blood drained. Every step he took was excruciatingly painful. Ballabh's shoulders bled each day. Since the arrival of the new slaves, the nightly routine had changed.

Instead of remembering and talking about their village and their moms, now they spent their scarce five hours of sleep lying face down, planning ways to please their master.

"Aatish," said Ballabh. "I think that if we stop laughing, our faces will become as inexpressive as those of the new slaves so we'll be more productive and better please the master."

Aatish was puzzled, not by the advice but because he realized that for months they had not laughed. There was nothing to smile about.

"Ballabh, don't you realize that we stopped laughing a long time ago?"

"It's not true, while I work, I laugh," he assured him, "I do it while ... while ..."

"While you daydream."

"Yes," Ballabh agreed, "I remember our village every now and then. I concentrate a lot on the memories to forget this life."

"I wonder if we'll ever be happy again."

"Aaagh," one of the new children complained. The newly arrived slaves had no names. They had a number tattooed on their right shoulders which distinguished them from the others.

Claudia Carbonell

Since neither of them spoke, not even when someone asked a question, they couldn't tell who had complained.

Ballabh covered his mouth with his grandmother's handkerchief so that his sobs would not be heard.

Meanwhile, Aatish pulled his feet out from under the tent. Exposing them to the intense cold was preferable to the thick fabric brushing against his lacerated soles.

Vivienne and her family were about to taste a delicious dinner before the Summit began. She could hardly believe her eyes. She constantly removed her glasses to clean them, touch her pearl necklace, and slip her fingers through her hair to make sure that no strand was out of order. Every now and then, she checked the five pages of her speech.

After writing and erasing it hundreds of times, she had finally printed it before driving to the airport. Had she counted all those tossed sheets of paper, she would surely have won the world record of most used paper.

While her nerves consumed her, it was easy to decipher the confident body language from the rest of the participants. They were cheering, toasting, and laughing.

Of course, she thought, *everyone here has had a lot of experience speaking in public. They are also very prepared, intelligent, and eloquent.*

She knew at least a dozen participants, like her favorite actor, Leonardo DiCaprio who was sitting three tables diagonal from her. At the moment, he was proposing a toast. Next to Leonardo sat Akie Abe, the First Lady of Japan, Ahmad Adhkar, founder of the Hult Prize, the largest student competition that generates social media awareness for worthy causes, Kavita Gupta, the famous entrepreneur, and others.

Vivienne spooned her cream of asparagus soup, but she had no appetite. She did not touch the roasted lamb dish with mint dressing garnished with cubed vegetables. As soon as the chocolate pudding arrived at the table, Turner was the first to attack it and ended up sticking his mouth into the plate. His lips and chin were smeared with pudding. The Pope, who was seated at the table in front of them, laughed. Turner tossed a kiss to him in the air, and Pope Francis opened his hand, clenched it, and placed it on his chest.

They all noticed Turner's feat and laughed out loud. Vivienne also laughed and forgot her fear for an instant. The waiters removed the plates and glasses from the tables. An elegant woman strolled to the dining room and announced, "Ladies and gentlemen, the Summit is about to begin.

Please follow me to the Conference Room."

"This is your great moment, Princess," Eric insisted. Unfortunately, this reminded her of all the time she had spent preparing her speech. It would never measure up to others. If she was a little older and academically prepared and had the fluency of expression like the other participants, her legs would not been shaking and her hands not been sweating so much. Head down, she stood up. There was a rush of icy air on the back of her neck. That as a result of the dumb haircut she got for the most important event of her life. She had wanted to look the best she ever had, but instead, looked her worst. Turner positioned himself next to her and their parents followed them.

She was holding the embodiment of terror between her fingers: those five pages of her speech. *I'll do terribly,* she thought. *Everyone will make fun of me. Oh, please, just stop thinking, Vivienne. Instead, occupy your mind on something else.* She started counting her steps ... "One, two, three, four ..."

"Why are you counting?" Turner whispered.

"My thoughts have sounds?" she asked, troubled.

"You're counting," he assured. He had some pudding on his upper lip. She wiped it with her index finger and, without thinking, cleaned her finger on the first page of the speech.

"Oh no, what have I done?" she asked aloud.

"Relax, my little girl," Alexandra said, and lifted her chin. "You're going to do just fine. Do not worry."

Vivienne wanted to tell her, *If I were you, I would have nothing to fear.* She slid her fingers through her hair and pulled on it. If magically her hair would stretch about five inches, she could hide her face and feel safer.

They walked into a conference room. It had the particular smell of a classroom on the first day of school; a combination of a room shut for several weeks and the whiff of pencil soot inside an electric sharpener. The long circular tables reminded her of the legend of King Arthur's Round Table. Some participants commented on the similarity of the room with that of the United Nations.

The lady who guided them to the room made another announcement, "Those of you who are speaking, find your nametags on the table." *Oh, I hope they forgot to make one for me! God please, make it disappear if they made me one by mistake,* Vivienne thought gazing up to the ceiling. Yet, Turner with a quick glance at the table, eyeballed his sister's nametag and proudly said, "I found your name, Vivi," while pointing to it.

Her stomach tightened in knots as she followed him to a tiny paper that bore her name.

Apparently, once everyone who had a tag was sitting in front of it, the announcer spoke again, "Now, family members, please find chairs. We should have enough to accommodate all of you."

Every attendee sat and were blabbing out loud. The woman sitting on the other side of Vivienne at this moment had her back turned and was having a lively conversation with the man next to her.

Pope Francis sat down on a table right in front of Vivienne's. He winked at her and inclined his head.

I'm about to disappoint you. Please forgive me, she thought and her eyes burned. Before the tears streamed down, she took the napkin from under a glass of water in front of her and inserted the tip of paper into her eyes. The edge of the napkin got soaked. She lifted her glass and took a sip of water. She had a hard time swallowing it. The liquid felt like a thick, bitter substance.

Dear God, take these nerves away from me, Vivienne thought.

Turner's eyes traveled all around the room. "We are the only children here!" he commented.

"You just realized that?" she said in disgust.

Her parents started talking to her. She knew they were giving her words of encouragement, but the noise and the strong throb of her heart extinguished their voices. On the other hand, an internal voice prevailed insisting, *Why won't the ground open up and swallow me?*

"We will now begin this Peace Summit. We will start with the First Lady of Japan, Akie Abe," said the announcer.

Vivienne would have preferred being deaf. As she listened to the First Lady's speech, her insecurity became more acute. She felt so small. Other fabulous speeches ensued, followed by fervent applause.

During the fourth dissertation, she fixed her eyes on her printed message. It was so simple. She stared at her parents and waited for the audience to applaud another brilliant speech.

"You didn't help me write it!" she blurted this out. She had kept that protest locked up between her throat and chest for a long time. A wave of hot blood rushed to her face. The table began to spin. She closed her eyes.

She heard Eric whispering, "Sweetie, the message had to come from your heart, not from our heads."

Claudia Carbonell

At the back of the first page was the picture of the two children who had taught her about child slavery. *Give me your strength. Unlike me, you guys are so brave.*

Exhaustion had won over Ballabh's desire to stay awake to devise ways to please his master. He was beat by such deep sleep that he had turned and was laying on his back. The burning sting on his shoulders and back woke him up with a jump.

Moonlight and the intense cold streamed through the glassless window and bathed their tent blanket and his brother's black hair. He stuck his icy feet under the tent. Once he barely brushed the soles of his feet with the stiff fabric, he moaned feeling the burning sting in them.

Vivienne felt a burning flare sensation over her shoulders. She shuddered.

"Now we will hear twelve-year-old Vivienne Harr," announced the lady, who had led them into the room.

It's my turn. My God and children, give me strength, she thought, staring at the photo of the slaves, feeling the rush of icy air on the back of her neck, and sensing the Pope's sweet gaze on her.

She adjusted her glasses. The letters looked blurry. She placed her index finger on the first line, eager to flatten the letters since they were jumping. The black spot of pudding she had cleaned from Turner's lips covered the first words. Turner, who was sitting next to her, laughed out loud.

She took a deep breath and started reading:

"Your Holiness Pope Francis, Cardinal Turkson, Mr. Van Dongen, distinguished guests, and family. I am honored to be here with you today. Thank you for having me."

A lump formed in her throat. She needed to let it go but she was afraid of swallowing saliva for fear of chocking.

"My name is Vivienne. I am 12 years old. I ask people to put their compassion into action—and to create peace and justice for those who need it most.

His Holiness Pope Francis has asked us to take action for the world's poorest people. Your Holiness, you and I share a common vision for humanity—and I will do what you have asked.

I am here as a voice for the 1.9 billion children in our world. I invite you to join me in taking action for the world's poorest people.

Your Holiness, I am reading your book *The Name of God is Mercy*. You talk so beautifully about mercy, inclusion, and action, in a way I could understand and apply in my life. I have become one of your biggest fans. I even follow you on Twitter now!

The audience laughed.

I love your song *Para que todos sean uno,* or *So We Can All Be One.* In it, you write: "So that all may be one. Gone are the walls, only the value of the encounter remains. That is the bridge to peace." I want to thank you, from the bottom of my heart, for helping others so much.

Your Holiness, you have said: "A little bit of mercy makes the world less cold and more just."

Turner continued with his nervous giggles.

Vivienne no longer heard them for the pain in her body was greater. She felt her shoulders lacerated. The pain dropped to her extremities. She couldn't figure out if it was due to her state of panic that the soles of her feet were burning as if they were stepping on burning coals. She stopped reading. She freed the message anchored in her heart, sat eyes directly on Pope Francis, and visualized those two children in the picture.

It is not enough to have them in front of me, she thought. She changed the mental image and placed herself and Turner there, contemplating the abyss and carrying those huge slabs of rocks.

"My story is about making the world less cold and more just. It is about the power of compassion in action.

When I was 8, I saw a photo of two brothers in a rock quarry in Nepal bracing themselves against the terrible burden of modern-day slavery. I thought slavery ended long ago. But it did not. I learned that there are 18 million children in slavery. That is 18 million too many.

When I looked at the photo, I said to my mom and dad: "Compassion is not compassion without action. We must do something."

I did not think of all the reasons why I could not (too young, too little). I thought of all the reasons why I must (help others...save the world!)

I set up my lemonade stand every day, rain or shine. After 173 days in a row, I raised $101,320 to eradicate child slavery, and I started a for-benefit business called "Make a Stand Lemon-aid," with profits going to a purpose: fighting child slavery.

You might wonder where my sense of social justice comes from! Like all good things, it starts with my family. I am proud to be from a family of immigrants. (In fact, my family is here today.)

My grandparents made great sacrifices for my parents, who made great sacrifices for me. If they had not, I might have had to sell lemons to help our family. Instead, I was able to sell lemonade to help our world.

But this is not about my story. It is about helping to write the stories of the many people who want to change the world. It is about empowering them to bring their courage, compassion, and commitment to serve the poor.

We are the millions of young people who want to help the bottom billion. My parents believed in me and look what happened.

Picture in your mind the future change-makers. They're out there right now. Imagine if we believe in them enough and support them enough—and love them enough—to where they believe in themselves enough to start their own business to serve the world's poorest people. Imagine the impact on humanity now...and forever.

I am grateful to be alive at a time in history when anyone anywhere can serve the world's poorest people in big and beautiful ways.

I am grateful to be alive at a time in history when we have a Pope like His Holiness Pope Francis, who is changing the world through mercy, inclusion, and action. I would like to finish with a quote by St. Ignatius of Loyola, who said:

Be generous to those in need. The man to whom our Lord has been liberal ought not to be stingy.

We shall one day find in Heaven as much rest and joy as we ourselves have dispensed in this life.

Thank you."

She finally reached the end of her speech. All the attendants, including Pope Francis, stood up to applaud her. They applauded for a minute and a half. Her speech was the most celebrated in the conference!

She tilted her head. This gave her the blessings and confidence needed. From now on, she would be bold and outspoken for her cause.

At the end of the conference, Pope Francis sat with the Harr family to talk.

"You touched me, young girl. Human pain afflicts me deeply but more so the suffering of the most underprivileged people and of all, child slavery could be the most vulnerable and forgotten. Thank you for giving them a voice."

She showed him the picture. He agreed to take a sum from the Vatican Fund to rescue a huge amount of child slaves. It would be a large sum of money. All the guests gathered around Vivienne. She had touched their hearts. The First Lady of Japan invited her to a conference at her country's Presidential House. Vivienne would give her speech about slavery.

For three years, Vivienne had gone to bed mainly after midnight because she preferred to watch documentaries about the most disadvantaged people in the world, instead of sleeping. Today, at the conclusion of the Peace Summit, she felt relieved to retire early to her room to rest. She had to recover.

The burning in the shoulders and soles on her feet persisted. At 7 p.m., she said goodbye to everyone and, escorted by her family, walked to her room. In an hour, Pope Francis had to give a sermon at the Jubilee Church and her parents were eager to attend.

Several guards escorted the Pope to his suite which was in front of hers.

Smiling, he waved goodbye to her.

Once inside and leaning against the door, she thought, *I did it. Guys, we made it.* Looking at the photo, she wished the slave boys good night.

Karishma, Aatish's and Ballabh's Mom, was holding stones in each hand and, with all her might. She yearned to raise her house again. She had spent 1,460 days in hell without her children. She was beginning another year without them, her fourth. It was January 1, 2017. Nothing could be more desolate.

"Oh, Mommy," she sobbed, "I thank God you didn't experience these two great tragedies, the earthquake and the loss of our little children." She stood up. Passing by dozens of tents reminded her of the years she spent as a nomad. She dragged her feet to the edge of the cliff. The waterfalls crashed against four boulders below the terrace where the remains of her house lay. Now, these remains could end up at any moment in a ravine which rushed to meet the Indrawati River. In the same way her husband's blood ended in that same stream.

Little ones, I've been four years without you. She thought about the moving bridge above the Indrawati. Her kids had crossed it so many times. I let you go because I wanted a better future for you.

Besides, the man of God promised to give you a good education, and also because I didn't want you to know about your Granny's death which happened the very morning you left. Why did you forget me? Don't you know that you are my life? My existence has now no purpose. Where are you little ones? Where are you?

Ballabh was lifting the fifth slab of the day. It weighed as much as his grief. He envied so much the new slaves. They were insensitive to fatigue, to the weight on their shoulders, to work, and to the weather changes. Besides, they were the only ones who were not punished by the master. He tried to lighten the pace but his shoulders were badly wounded. Blood had stained Grandpa's shirt. The band above his head had formed a ditch in his skull, and it hurt. Ouch! It hurt as much as his feet. The corns were split on his big toes, his medial, and his heels. His brother's were worse off.

They were barefoot. Their sandals had fallen apart long ago. He collapsed on the ground and pulled the backpack off his back. He settled his forehead on his knees. His vertebrae cracked like broken bones. He felt defeated. He could never be like the newly arrived slaves.

I'm just a child, he thought.

Aatish was already setting foot on the peak of the mountain when he saw him.

"Have you gone mad?" he shouted, "If the master sees you, he will kill you!"

"Aatish, I can't bear this any longer. My shoulders; oh, my feet." He didn't have the strength to keep talking. He curled into the fetal position and closed his eyes.

"You didn't eat today and last night you barely tasted your dinner. That's why you're lacking strength. Look at the new slaves, they eat a lot. You must imitate them. We must ... Ballabh, Ballabh, are you listening?"

He had fallen asleep. He looked so peaceful. Aatish pulled out his backpack, placed it on top of his brother's pack, and carried him. The new slaves watched them in horror. He approached a eucalyptus tree and, leaning against the trunk, he let himself fall to the ground. He placed Ballabh's head on his thighs. He noticed the fabric on the shoulders of their grandfather's blue shirt was drenched in blood and was stuck to his skin. He did not want to pull it off for fear of hurting him even more.

"Sleep," he suggested, "I'll stay with you." He was prepared to receive double punishment. But first, he would get down on his knees before the master and beg him to beat him up as much as he wanted, but to not put a finger on his brother. He was too hurt and needed to recover. He would.

He was strong; more than he. They would soon yield as much as the new slaves. It was only a matter of time.

"Aatish, keep working," Ballabh begged, halfway opening his eyes, "or the master will also kill you."

"We'll then die together. We'll be with Dad and Grandpa."

"You won't. You have to go back to the village and live with the Moms," urged Ballabh.

"Don't be silly. Without you, I won't go anywhere. Now, shut up and sleep." Ballabh had to sleep soundly so he would not hear the blows or the bullets. He hoped the master got it over quickly so his brother would not witness it. He stretched his neck and peered down the mountain. He had not stretched his neck in a long time. The vertebrae sounded as if they had broken out and a spasmodic pain followed.

A woman was speaking with the master and a van was parked next to his truck. They walked into the former barn. Now it housed the slaves. Minutes later they marched out. The lady wrote something on a piece of paper. The children did not imagine that she was writing a check.

Now Devang was blowing his whistle. He did it every time he wanted to talk to them. The slaves who were up in the mountain began their descent. Those below lined up against the wall of the recruiting building.

"Oh no! Ballabh, wake up, wake up, we must go down the mountain. Be strong. There's a slave buyer down the hill and I don't want them to separate us."

Ballabh opened his eyes halfway and shut them again. Aatish realized he could not force him to do anything. He picked him up and started the descent. He turned to set eyes on the backpacks. They were left on the ground. He descended slowly, watching each step. He had memorized every dent and line of those rocky steps. It seemed they had stepped on them their entire lives. A redhead monal rushed down the steps and brushed his feet with its wings.

His brother weighed less than half of a slab but it was different to carry the weight on the back than on front. He felt that at any moment they would roll down the mountain face first.

"I swear Ballabh, if the buyer decides to pick one of us instead of choosing us together, I'd rather die." Apparently, he had whispered that cry. He wanted to cry, but now his eyes were as dry as his faith.

Claudia Carbonell

The monal stood on the first step at the foot of the mountain. Once Aatish was about to set foot on this last stair, the monal took flight and landed on the vehicle. The winged creature was shining. Its crest fluttered from side to side with the breeze and the flutters of its wings seemed to be shedding light.

The woman began to speak and a man who stepped out of her van translated her heavenly words:

"Kids, you are now free."

The New Year's celebration had exhausted the Harr family. Today, Vivienne, Turner, Zenobia, Eva, Savanah, Franco, and Rebecca, were playing in the treehouse.

It was so crowded that Buddy couldn't fit in. Down below, he barked at them, begging to be taken up. Vivienne was narrating her experience of the trip to the Vatican, the conference, and the proceeds she helped raise: $10 billion. The Pope had approved this amount to free millions of child slaves.

"That's a whole lot of money!" shouted Franco as he grabbed another apple from the tree.

"Vivienne, did you find out what happened to the children in the photo?" asked Eva.

"Oh yes, they had a happy ending," Vivienne replied. "It turns out they were two brothers named Aatish and Ballabh Singh. They returned to their village and were reunited with their mother. The village has a strange name and now I can't remember it..."

"The village was destroyed by an earthquake, remember?" Turner intervened.

"Yes, but it was rebuilt with the money collected," Vivienne assured.

"And now a writer called Daddy and said she was going to write a book about Vivienne. Ha ha ha!" said Turner, bursting in nervous giggles.

"Oh wow! There's going to be a book about your life story, Vivienne?" asked Zenobia, her jaw dropping in astonishment. "My gosh, do you know what the title will be?"

"The writer said it was going to be called, *The Little Girl and the Pope*," replied Vivienne as she took a deep breath. Her shoulders felt light now. Her feet were rested. She was breathing easily and the breeze on the back of her neck had the warmth of the breath of all the rescued children.

Claudia Carbonell

About the Author

Claudia Carbonell was born in Cali, Colombia and began writing short stories when she was seventeen years old. At nineteen, her writing career officially began after being published in a popular Ecuadorian newspaper called El Meridiano (The Meridian), where she worked as a columnist. She continued on a course of writing and study which led her to the US where she has earned many degrees and awards.

She has never stopped writing and her life work, which is 20 years in the making, is found in an incredible nine-book fantasy series, appropriately named, *The Magical Series,* written for children and teens. This series contains eight books plus a book of short supplementary stories.

Claudia Carbonell

The series is rich in themes which the author feels most passionate about such as the human impact on the ecology, especially on her beloved rain forest and the issue of animal cruelty. She also loves to describe the diverse variety of fauna and flora, many of which are medicinal and threatened along with the overall living ecology of the forest.

She expands and exposes these themes and dangers to the planet in her stories through the beautiful filter of fantasy, "from the animals' point of view," as they strive to survive the destruction and abuse of humans. Of equal impact, is the environmental deterioration and "Man's" (as he is referred to) ambition which destroys the forests, jungles and contaminates water sources. Make believe fantasy creatures and others created by the author, make their debut through multiple worlds and exalt their messages throughout the series. The author's sense of humor and unique 'voice,' is present on each page of her books. Without a doubt, this work is not only entertaining for the young and old alike but educates the reader in a heart felt manner.

Claudia has also given herself to the mission of writing another series of books titled, The Magical Heroes. This series is about children who are changing the world. Her goal with both series is to encourage her Readers to love our planet and to direct them to also be part of this movement to improve the society we live in through enhanced awareness of the atrocities taking place in the world, from child slavery, the destruction of the Rainforest and animal and plant species.

Claudia is also passionate about helping people achieve their goals. She is a clinical hypnotherapist, family couple therapist, and a life coach. Claudia lives in Southern California with her husband, Aaron and her mother, Lola. Her two children: Brigitte, and Andrew Phillip, live close enough to once in a while allow her to share with their adorable Chihuahua, Zoe.

Claudia Carbonell

Other Books from the Author

The Tree of Life
Enlightened State

The Magical Series:

The Magical House
The Magical Forest

Coming soon from The Magical Series:

The Magical Farm
The Magical Jungle
The Magical Ocean
The Magical Glaciers
Introduction to the Magical Kingdom
The Magical Kingdom
Techno City

Coming soon from The Magical Heroes:

Zenobia and her Dolls

Life on the Brink of a Lovely Melody

A Letter to God

Claudia Carbonell

The Magical Series Reviews

The Magical House, by Claudia Carbonell, combines the poetry of language with the freshness of animal-humanity perspective. In this feast of delectable characters, her delicious prose portrays credible and human-like characters... though they travel the world on four legs. The plot captures us from the first moment. The adventures of Dolly the bear, and her cubs Spunky and Pink, don't allow time to set the book aside. On the other hand, the aristocratic and vegetarian rabbit (Sir Trottingham Mathew III), joins the bear family. And then there is Loretta, a lap dog with a sad story of unrewarded faithfulness... This is a fable of the love of freedom, independence, friendship and family. The bear cubs, their adoptive mother and the rest of the well-crafted characters, present us with conflicts with which all (young and those not so young) can easily identify with. Now we hope for the continuation of this adventure!

Teresa Doval, bestseller author: *A Girl like Che Guevara* (Soho Press, 2004), *Posesas de la Havana* (PurePlay Press, 2004) and Death of a Murcian (Anagram, 2006), finalist of the Herald prize in Spain in November of the 2006.

Claudia Carbonell

As an author who read *The Magical House* by Claudia Carbonell, I simply cannot stop admiring how she has combined the love of animals, the protection of our world, and most shockingly, the inclemency of adults for not conserving theirs and the animal world. Besides this, there are segments in the story charged with a poetic prose which will delight children and adult readers, alike. The dialogue among animals is simply delicious.

Margarita Noguera, author of *Entre Arcoiris y Nubarrones*.

In *The Magical House, The Magical Forest* and *The Magical Farm*, Claudia Carbonell has created charming and fascinating worlds. And what rarity is it to find fantasy-completely convincing! As a professor, I admire her ability to make everything seem so natural; as a writer, I feel a little more than jealous!

--Kevin Jones, D.A. (Doctor in Arts) Professor/Counselor of The Union Institute & University. Books: *Bikeu* (poems), Shoestring Press, 2003; *William Wantling: A Commemoration* (Ed.), Babbitt's Books, 1994.

Claudia Carbonell reveals with her prodigious imagination the lives of animals in her second book, The Magical Forest. The exquisite sensitivity of the author blooms in the examples she gives, suggesting to her readers the distinction between good and evil.

On its own or as part of the Magical Series, it is a source of wisdom and pleasure for young children because of their age and for adults as well.

Graciela Lecube-Chavez Actress, writer, publisher, translator and director of commercials. Best actress, 2006. Winner of Life Achievement Award of H.O.L.A. (Hispanic Association of Latin Actors), 2004.

Allegorical fantasies surround the Magical Series where freedom and love take you to different horizons of dreams where illusion flies like an eagle in the sky. Taken by the author's hand, you will be transported to a magical world.

Maricela R. Loaeza author of *Poemas por amor* and *Poemas ineditos Antologia de bohemios por amor*.

The Magical Series is a delicious combination of fantasy and a deep love of Nature. Spellbound by the images and the characters, the reader is taken inside a plot of unexpected twists and turns that touches his consciousness and forces him to question himself about the human attacks against the natural world - the animals, the forests, the water. This work, in which the mastery of the author's narrative and pedagogical abilities are interlaced admirably, is an extensive and loving fable, very pertinent in this apocalyptic dawn of the 21st century, and whose moral, especially if young readers are the interpreters, will unquestionably agree in our obligation that we have to take action if we want to survive. Claudia Carbonell has the unquestionable narrative skill and the ability to model characters that will bring to mind to the astonished reader a few of the greatest creators of children's literature: Lewis Carroll, Hans Christian Andersen, Michael Ende, Walt Disney... We "voraciously" await for the continuation of this wonderful Magical Series.

—Roberto Pinzón-Galindo Editor of the Institute Caro & Cuervo, Bogotá Colombia

Claudia Carbonell

184

Claudia Carbonell

Made in the USA
Columbia, SC
27 July 2024

39222966R00112